CHINESE COMMERCIAL NEGOTIATING STYLE

CHINESE
COMMERCIAL
NEGOTIATING
STYLE

Lucian Pye

Oelgeschlager, Gunn & Hain, Publishers, Inc.
Cambridge, Massachusetts

Athenäum
Königstein/Ts., West Germany

International Standard Book Number: 0-89946-168-9 cloth
                                     0-89946-171-9 paper

Library of Congress Catalog Card Number: 82-14136

Printed in the U.S.A.

Library of Congress Cataloging in Publication Data

Chinese commercial negotiating style.

Includes index.
1. Negotiation in business—China.   I. Title.
HD58.5.P9   1982   658.8′48′0951   82-14136
ISBN   0-89946-168-9
         0-89946-171-9 (pbk.)

Jacket/cover design by Clifford Stoltze.
Chinese calligraphy by Sidney L. Tai.

CONTENTS

v

PREFACE

This study analyzes the style of the Chinese in their negotiations with American businessmen. What can be learned from the experiences of businessmen should also be of value for government-to-government negotiations, even though there are substantial differences between commercial and diplomatic relationships. At present, both Beijing and Washington wish to put their adversary competition behind them and seek a more cooperative and complementary relationship. If we can better understand the Chinese style of negotiating in the commercial realm, we should be able to avoid misunderstandings and achieve desired goals in the political realm.

The analysis is based upon extensive informal interviews and conversations conducted by the author with Americans engaged in China trade, most of whom are residents of Hong Kong. To control for American cultural biases, he carried out similar interviews with Japanese traders and officials in Tokyo and Osaka. Even with promises of complete confidentiality it was difficult for the businessmen to tell stories that might be traced back to them. Nor were they inclined to engage in abstract analysis based on generalities; they were comfortable only when speaking from concrete examples. Consequently, the respondents were inclined to skip over difficulties and concentrate on success stories. Even so, enough information was collected to make it possible to describe and analyze the negotiating practices in the China trade.

This study was completed for The Rand Corporation under the Project AIR FORCE research project, "China's Strategic and Regional Roles in Asian Security."

SUMMARY

This study analyzes Chinese commercial negotiating practices for two reasons. The first is to minimize future misunderstandings in such activities, and the second reason is to provide guidance for government-to-government negotiations. The procedure was to interview American businessmen and bankers with extensive experience in the China trade, and, so as to control for American cultural factors, to interview comparable Japanese bankers and businessmen.

The way most Sino-American negotiations are initiated generally sets in motion a process that helps the Chinese achieve their preferred strategies and tactics. The novelty and the status associated with visiting China frequently compels chief executive officers to be the first in their firms to engage in talks with the Chinese, without waiting for subordinates to prepare the ground. Consequently, foreigners tend to be very obliging in following the Chinese practice of seeking initial agreement on very general principles, without clarification on the specific details.

Subsequently, when middle level executives must work out the details of the contract they usually discover that the Chinese will first use to practical advantage the agreed principles that the Americans took to be mere ritual statements, most often by suggesting that the other party has not lived up to the "spirit" of the principles. The obvious analogy in state-to-state relations is the opening of China by Dr. Henry Kissinger and President Richard Nixon and the subsequent frequent Chinese charges that Washington was not living up to the "spirit" of the Shanghai Communique or the Joint Communique on the Establishment of Diplomatic Relations.

In commercial transactions, agreement on principles usually takes the form of letters of intent or protocols, the purpose of which often mystifies American businessmen because the Chinese will readily cancel the details of such agreements while insisting that the "spirit" must be maintained.

The Chinese reject the typical American notion that agreement is best sought by focusing on specific details and avoiding discussions of generalities. They prefer instead agreeing on the general principles of the relationship before dealing with troublesome details. The Chinese use the occasion of such preliminary exchanges on generalities to size up the other party and to determine how vulnerable he may be, especially whether he lacks patience. For Chinese officials, displaying impatience is a major sin, and they are masters of the art of stalling while keeping alive the other party's hopes.

Furthermore, the Chinese are skilled at using their role as hosts to control the timing of meetings, the arrangement of agendas, and the general pacing of negotiations. They are able, moreover, to insinuate that it is the foreign businessman who, in coming to China, is seeking favors from the Chinese. The problems of getting visas, arranging for the invitation to Beijing, and finding the appropriate officials there with whom to deal all contribute to American anxieties about doing the wrong thing; hence, when problems arise, Americans are prone to suspect that they are the ones at fault.

Although the Chinese place much store on friendship and have shown themselves sensitive to the political views of other parties, they tend to attach even greater importance to the prestige and reputation of the various competitors, preferring to deal with only the "best"—a traditional cultural trait that has been reinforced by the current bureaucratic need of officials to avoid all possible criticisms.

In actual negotiations, the Chinese usually arrange for the other party to show his hand first. Because they see negotiations as partly information gathering operations, they frequently play off competitors against each other to get the maximum technical intelligence out of the American's presentation "seminars." (Americans apparently derive great personal satisfaction from teaching the Chinese all they seek to know and are rarely offended by the Chinese attitude that "Your proprietary secrets are 'private property' and hence vulgar, selfish matters, while ours are 'state secrets,' matters of honor." The Japanese, who once had a reputation for copying others, now ironically have a greater awareness of the value of knowledge and therefore protect their proprietary secrets more carefully.)

The Chinese believe that patience is a value in negotiations, particularly with impatient Americans, and they freely use stalling tactics and delays. Their use of time also reflects lack of experience, bureaucratic problems, and subordinate's fear of criticism from above. Once an agreement has been reached, however, it is the Chinese who often become impatient for deliveries by the foreign firm.

Chinese negotiators can be both obstinate and flexible in that they may be very tenacious in holding to their "principles" while surprisingly flexible about "details." They are quick to point out any "mistakes" by the other party, and they expect that others will be put on the defensive by such errors. They genuinely believe that people will be shattered by the shame of their faults, and they can be very persistent in making an issue over trivial slip-ups and misstatements. In the middle of negotiations Chinese have no hesitation in presenting what they must understand are unacceptable demands. They hint, however, that the demand can be tabled if the other side will make only modest concessions. They may also use extreme language to gain symbolic victories.

American negotiators tend to prize their ability to be understanding and to make allowances for the problems and limitations of Chinese negotiators. In contrast, Chinese steel themselves against feelings of empathy and are quick to move aggressively if they sense that the other party has problems. The Chinese generally reject the principle of compromise and prefer instead to stress mutual interests. Once the Chinese believe that there is an agreed mutual interest they have every expectation that it is only right for the better off or richer partner to bear the heavier burden without protest. For various reasons, Chinese seem to feel that the world sees them as somehow "special," giving rise to a peculiar revival of the traditional Middle Kingdom complex, which leads Chinese to expect special consideration and treatment.

Chinese negotiating teams tend to be large, but lines of authority can be diffuse and vague. Technical specialists and representatives of end users may aggressively take part in the deliberations but turn out not to have commensurate influence on final decisions. Chinese negotiators are often unsure not only of their mandates but also of the probable decisions of their superiors; therefore they may inaccurately signal the state of progress of negotiations. Warm and progressively more friendly meetings can lead to disappointing outcomes, while apparently disinterested negotiators can suddenly announce that a positive agreement is possible.

Chinese often find it awkward to use formal sessions for clarification purposes, and many prefer informal exchanges between formal sessions. They will privately seek out any ethnic Chinese associated with the American team, who they believe are naturally sympathetic to China. Because of these considerations the Japanese always insist on having Chinese-speaking Japanese present at all negotiations.

Chinese negotiators often seem ambivalent in their feelings toward foreign negotiators because they are torn between distrust of foreigners and fascination with foreign technologies, which they believe can miraculously transform their society. Their approach in working out this ambivalence is to seek, probably unconsciously, relationships in which the foreign party will feel solicitous toward China, thus implicitly becoming a protector, and more a superior than an equal. Precisely for this reason the Chinese often seek to compensate by being authoritative in tangential matters.

In contrast to American practices, the Chinese do not treat the signing of a contract as signaling a completed agreement; rather, they conceive of the relationship in longer and more continuous terms, and they will not hesitate to suggesting modifications immediately on the heels of an agreement. Their expectation is that agreements will set the stage for a growing relationship in which it will be proper for China to make increasing demands on the other party. This Chinese view of unending negotiation also makes them insensitive to the possibility that canceling contracts may cause trouble in the relationship.

The most elementary rules for negotiating with the Chinese are: (1) practice patience; (2) accept as normal prolonged periods of no movement; (3) control against exaggerated expectations, and discount Chinese rhetoric about future prospects; (4) expect that the Chinese will try to influence by shaming; (5) resist the temptation to believe that difficulties may have been caused by one's own mistakes; and (6) try to understand Chinese cultural traits, but never believe that a foreigner can practice them better than the Chinese.

ACKNOWLEDGMENTS

A pledge of confidentiality was made to those who were gracious enough to give their time to this project. Therefore, it is not possible to acknowledge by name all of those who provided data for this study. In the field of banking, negotiators from four major American financial institutions concerned with promoting China trade shared the benefits of their experiences. Officials of three large U.S. telecommunications and space satellite firms discussed their negotiating relationships. Several aircraft parts wholesalers and light aircraft dealers also provided information. The field of manufacturing was covered by two giant enterprises and a large number of specialized firms in such areas as printing presses, textile machinery, chemical plants, cable and wire, machine tools, presses and dies, and optics; smaller enterprises involved mostly Chinese exports such as wearing apparel, and dealers in Chinese arts and crafts. In the raw materials and commodities category, there were traders in tobacco, metals, pig bristles, and cotton.

Finally, and possibly most helpful of all, were two professional consultants on doing business with China, Thomas Gorman of China Consultants International, and Lynn Edinger of Extell, Inc., and officials of the American Chamber of Commerce in Hong Kong.

In Japan, the most helpful information came from two large trading companies, specialized electronic firms, officials of the China Trade Division of the Keidanren (the Japanese Federation of Economic Organizations), the Japan-China Trade Association, the Japan External Trade Organization, editors of several trade and economic publications, including the *China Newsletter* and the Nihon Keiza-Shinbun, and officials at the Ministry of Foreign Affairs and the Ministry of International Trade and Industry (MITI).

In Hong Kong I was graciously assisted by officials of the American Consulate General, and in particular, by Consul-General Thomas P. Shoesmith, Colonel James M. Reed, Jr., USAF, and Gilbert Donahue. John Dolfin and members of his staff at the Hong Kong Universities Service Center were once again most considerate. Roger Sullivan, Charles W. Freeman, and Michael Witunski reviewed the manuscript and made numerous suggestions for improvements. At Rand I got strong moral and intellectual support from Richard H. Solomon, helpful criticism from Jonathan Pollack, K. C. Yeh, and Paul F. Langer, and cheerful administrative support from Mary Yanokawa. Lola

Klein carefully typed and retyped the many drafts. Mary Pye substantially improved my style, and Helen B. Turin thoughtfully and skillfully edited the final work.

Neither the organizations nor the persons who have been so helpful should be thought of as necessarily sharing my interpretations, and any failings remaining are mine alone.

I. THE SOURCES OF DIFFICULTIES

At present, relations between the United States and China are progressing remarkably well. Trade between the two countries rose rapidly in 1980 to a total of $4.9 billion, more than double the previous year's total, and euphoria for China, a form of "China fever" or "Marco Poloitis," persists in America and is reciprocated by a Chinese public seemingly dazzled by all things American. (Europeans tell of being asked in China whether they are American, and when they explain that they are not, the response is "Ah, too bad, what a pity.")

It is in the spirit of hoping to prevent later disillusionment and bad feelings that I have set out to identify and analyze a potential source of trouble, misunderstandings that can arise from differences in commercial negotiating styles and practices.

It is certainly a paradox that businessmen should have become key actors in building a new relationship between capitalist America and Communist China. Yet as long as corporate executives, entrepreneurs, bankers, and traders have become so important in shaping the new relationship, it is desirable to make sure that the process of negotiating, which always has an element of tension, not become in itself a cause of bad feelings.

Also, what we can learn about Chinese negotiating practices in dealing with the American private sector may be of help for public sector negotiations with Chinese officials. Before the current opening of relations with China, American officials had considerable, but generally unhappy, experiences in negotiating with the Chinese. As far back as early 1966, Assistant Secretary of State for Far Eastern Affairs William Bundy made the point that despite the absence of formal diplomatic relations, the U.S. government "had had the longest and most direct dialogue of any Western nation with Peking."[1] Most of the negotiating sessions before 1971 were of a harsh adversary nature, as at Panmunjom and in the Geneva and Warsaw Ambassadorial Talks.[2] Yet, as the late Ambassador Kenneth T. Young thoughtfully argued, even the adversary form of negotiations could be, and was to some degree, used by the United States to move

---

[1]*Department of State Bulletin,* Vol. LIV, No. 1392, February 28, 1966.

[2]For analyses of Chinese negotiating styles under hostile adversary conditions, see: Admiral Turner Joy, *How Communists Negotiate,* Macmillan, New York, 1955; and Arthur H. Dean, "What It Is Like to Negotiate with the Chinese," *New York Times Magazine,* October 30, 1966.

toward a more constructive relationship with China.[3] The political climate since normalization is, of course, radically different as amity has replaced enmity; but if the new positive conditions are to be preserved, the very process central to day-to-day business in both the private and public sectors, that of negotiations, must not become a cause of irritation and misunderstanding.

Although the conventional view among both businessmen and diplomats is that negotiation is the act of maximizing mutual interests to the end that all parties benefit, in practice it is easy for the process to arouse distrust and the competitive spirit of adversaries. It is commonplace to say that as long as parties are talking they are not likely to fight, but that is clearly not always true; sophisticated observers recognize that the very process of talking can exacerbate tensions, and this is why there was a growing interest, especially at the beginning of the Cold War, in the merits of tacit over explicit negotiations.[4] Yet if relations between the United States and China are to progress in the spirit of amity, it will be necessary to have widespread negotiations in many realms, without undue strain.

Sober heads in America and in China have warned that euphoria may give way to disappointment precisely because of exaggerated expectations about the promise of both the China market and the foreign policy payoffs of the new relationship. Fault-finding is likely to be a consequence of the inevitable coming down to earth that must soon occur as Americans and Chinese go beyond the stage of symbolic ties to the strains of mundane realities.

As China's relations with the West and Japan take on greater substantive content, a critical factor determining evaluations of China will be the reports of Chinese negotiating practices. The kind of reputation a country develops through its bargaining and negotiating practices has profound consequences on how it will be treated in the world of nation-states.[5] In the recent past, the Chinese established an unambiguous reputation for being a tough adversary negotiating country; and before that, Chinese diplomats brought disproportionate prestige to their weak and divided country through their shrewd bargaining. At present, the steady flow of Chinese commercial negotiations will decisively determine Beijing's bargaining reputation

---

[3]*Negotiating with the Chinese Communists*, McGraw-Hill, New York, 1968. This key volume in the Council of Foreign Affairs series "The United States and China in World Affairs" was designed to explore the record of adversary negotiations with the Chinese in the hope of finding ways for improving relations between the two countries.

[4]The pioneer studies of the advantages of tacit over explicit negotiations are: Thomas Schelling, *The Strategy of Conflict*, Harvard University Press, Cambridge, 1960; and Fred Charles Iklé, *How Nations Negotiate*, Praeger, New York, 1967.

[5]On the importance of bargaining reputations, see Iklé (1967), Chapter 6.

for the next phase of history. Will the Chinese be able to revive their historic image of being shrewd but honest negotiators? Or will they prove to have thin skins, easy to take offense and hypersensitive to any fancied national slights? Will they be aboveboard and open, or will they bluff and threaten? Will they damage their reputation by trying to be too clever? Will they exploit the gullible but protest too much when they are tested? Will they honor their contracts?

The future reputation of China is going to be colored by the continuing effects of her historic reputation, her current practices, and the success of China and the West in surmounting the difficulties inherent in the present stage of reestablishing extensive relationships. China is in the process of establishing a new reputation in negotiating, and its image will decisively affect the extent to which it will realize its potential of being a major asset for international peace and stability.

THE CHANGING CONTEXT OF COMMERCIAL NEGOTIATIONS

A brief review of the recent changes in Chinese trade policies will provide a helpful background. Foreign traders have not been particularly influenced by the existing realities of the Chinese economy, they have rather been inspired by their dreams of the future, which have been either self-generated or produced by Chinese political rhetoric. It is surprising how much foreign expectations have been out of synchronization with the realities of the Chinese economy, and that has created negotiating problems. There have been times when the foreign traders were cautious and the Chinese expansive, but more often the traders were exuberant while the Chinese were beset with problems that they understandably preferred not to publicize. In retrospect it is amazing that euphoria about the long-run prospects of China trade has survived these several phases of short-run contradictory desires. Four such phases are readily identifiable.

For present purposes, the first phase in negotiating relations began with the Kissinger-Nixon overtures to China shortly after the end of the Cultural Revolution and lasted until 1976 and the death of Mao and the "smashing" of the Gang of Four. During this period most substantive trade was limited to the semi-annual meetings of the Canton Trade Fair. Negotiations tended to be sharply focused on specific commodities and export items to China. There was still considerable political by-play, and the politics of traders at times seemed as important as what they had to sell or what they wanted to buy. Questions about whether the trader had operations in Taiwan at times became troublesome. Larger American firms and especially banks wanted to break out of the confines of the trade fairs and establish direct contacts with officials in Beijing. (During this phase American commercial relations with China uncomfortably resembled Sino-British relations in the early 19th century when the Chinese wanted to keep the foreigners contained in Canton but the foreigners wanted contacts at the capital in Peking.)

Although Japanese trade was more extensive and Sino-Japanese relationships more established, the pattern during this period was much the same. Most trade was conducted by "friendly trading companies" that were prepared to support Chinese political rhetoric and abstain from any dealings with Taiwan. From 1963 to 1968—that is, from the period of economic recovery after the Great Leap to the end of the Cultural Revolution—business transactions were conducted under the Liao-Takasaki Trade Agreement, a privately negotiated "treaty," which largely determined what would be traded by whom. Then after the Cultural Revolution until 1974, another more open but still privately negotiated memorandum set the rules of trade. In January 1974, the two governments signed an official agreement and trade was opened up to more than just the previous "friendly" firms. Volume did not greatly expand however. Japanese negotiations during this first phase were characterized on the one hand by numerous small firms, each anxious to preserve its monopoly and hence constantly pressing the Chinese to "remember politics," and on the other hand by the exploratory efforts of larger firms to achieve some form of depoliticized trade.

American and Japanese traders believed during this phase that if they could only avoid all the political rocks and shoals they should be able to find clear sailing for reasonably profitable trade. In the negotiating process they found the Chinese to be extremely sensitive to national slights and still addicted to propagandistic slogans and code words.

A second distinct phase in commercial relations extended from the death of Mao to the announcement of Sino-American normalization in the fall of 1978. During this period there was a rise in expectations among American traders, fed by ever more grandiose Chinese rhetoric about the Four Modernizations, but dampened by repeated disappointments over the signing of actual contracts. The Chinese Ten-Year-Plan for 1976-1985—which was belatedly announced by Chairman Hua Guofeng in February 1978, hence sometimes called the Eight-Year-Plan—triggered off great excitement among those anxious to enter the China Trade. In particular, it stimulated inquiries and efforts to open negotiations from large suppliers and banks who were impressed with the plan's goals of 120 large-scale industrial projects (including 10 iron and steel complexes, 9 nonferrous metals enterprises, 8 large-scale coal combines, 10 new oil and natural gas fields, 30 major hydroelectric stations, 6 new trunk railroads, and 5 key harbors), a doubling of steel production to reach 60 million tons a year, and a 50 percent increase in annual food production, which would mean doubling the growth rate of the previous decade. The estimates of the Chinese leaders that capital investments would total at least $600 billion between 1978 and 1986 made the foreign traders and bankers all the more determined to get into the China market as quickly as possible.[6]

When American trade with China did not grow along with these dramatic projections for the Four Modernizations, most American traders rationalized the lack of progress by believing that expansion would come with the normalization of diplomatic relations. Thus, the announcements from Washington and Beijing on December 15, 1978 that normalization would take place on January 1 of the next year stimulated a new burst of enthusiasm.

When Japan and China normalized diplomatic relations in 1972, the growth in their trade failed to live up to the dreams of those who wanted to partake in China's expected rapid industrialization. Although normalization had apparently set the stage for government-to-government arrangements about trade, the Japanese, exploiting their unique ability to blend the interests of government and industry, fell back upon a formula for a private agreement that carried government approval. In February 1978, Yoshihiro Inayama, president of the Japan-China Association on Economy and Trade, signed a long-term comprehensive trade agreement with Chinese Foreign Trade Vice-Minister Liu Ximen, envisioning a goal of two-way trade of $20 billion a year by 1985. During the first four years the trade was to be tilted in favor of Japanese exports to China of heavy industry plants and equipment, technologies, and construction materials; the last four years would emphasize Chinese exports of crude oil, coal, and other raw materials.

In August 1978, Japanese traders were further encouraged by the signing of the Sino-Japanese Treaty of Peace and Amity, which had long been stalled by the Chinese demand for an "anti-hegemony" clause. At just about the same time that American traders were preparing to mount a more active campaign in the wake of normalization, the Japanese also felt that they at last could expect to realize the

---

[6]For an excellent summary of these ambitious Chinese goals of development, see Richard Baum, "Introduction," in Richard Baum (ed.), *China's Four Modernizations: The New Technological Revolution,* Westview Press, Boulder, Colo., 1980.

benefits of a modernizing China. There was indeed a spectacular rise in the signing of contracts with Japanese firms. From February 1978 to January 1979 formal agreements were reached that would have totaled some $9 billion in two-way trade. Both Chinese and Japanese hurriedly negotiated contracts that would have more than used up all available Chinese capital. The Japanese rationalized that the Chinese should not be deterred because they could accept the offers of the international banking community to provide China with almost $30 billion in credits.

Thus, during the second phase, both Americans and Japanese were reacting to unrealistic Chinese propaganda about the Four Modernizations, while the Chinese were still groping for the boundaries of reality behind the smoke-screen of their ambitious rhetoric.

Beginning about January 1979, a third phase found the foreign traders and the Chinese completely out of step, but neither was ready to admit that such could be the case. At the very moment when the American and Japanese businessmen and bankers were ready to move ahead with an expected dramatic surge of activity, the Chinese leaders undertook a detailed reexamination of the prospects of their economy and concluded that they had taken leave of reality. The Ten-Year-Plan was scrapped and replaced by what was announced to be a three-year period of readjustment.

Chinese behavior sent two contradictory sets of signals to the foreign business community; one it chose to ignore, but it placed exaggerated faith in the other. The first set of signals involved the freezing of most contracts; some eventually were revived, but others were totally canceled. In mid-February the Chinese, without warning, suspended 23 major contracts for the purchase of various types of large plants and equipment from Japan.[7] The Chinese also turned their backs on innumerable letters of intent they had signed. These signals might have been expected to dash cold water on the enthusiasms of the foreign traders.

Yet the optimism of the traders remained firm until the fall of 1979 —they did not want to see their dreams shattered, and they found renewed hope in Beijing's talk of introducing new joint venture laws and a commercial code that would include promising tax laws and arbitration arrangements. Although Beijing was vague about the pace of such legal progress, the traders chose to read such hints as counters to the negative signals of the canceled contracts. Furthermore, elements within the Chinese bureaucracy gave added life to the

---

[7]For a subsequent Japanese interpretation of the significance of these Chinese moves, see Keiji Samejima, "Economic Readjustment: Its Meaning for China," *China Newsletter*, No. 24, December 1979, pp. 16-23.

vision of the growth of Chinese heavy industry by agreeing in March 1979 to extend the Sino-Japanese private trade agreement to 1990 and to increase the goal of two-way trade to a volume of $50-60 billion a year. Consequently, euphoria continued to rise even as the Chinese leaders were turning away from emphasis on heavy industry, for which they would have to buy machinery from abroad, and deciding to invest more in agriculture and light consumer industries. These moves might require some imports, but they would quickly put China into competition with American and Japanese investments in the ASEAN and other developing countries.

It was not until October-November 1979 that American enthusiasm about China trade began to approach reality for the first time. It was no longer possible to ignore the Chinese down-playing of heavy industry when they suddenly broke off negotiations with U.S. Steel Corporation after just having signed a protocol with a contract value of more than $1 billion. Many American firms decided to review their investments of time and money into opening the doors of China trade and concluded that if the Chinese were to make "readjustments," then they should do the same. Some major American companies chose to pull back entirely and await the maturing of the China market. Many of the more speculative operators turned to more promising fields.

Yet the dream of the China market proved irresistible, and by January 1980 there was a new swelling of hope among those who were still committed. The stimulus this time was certain Chinese actions that seemed to imply a more "pragmatic" approach. These developments included the new practice of allowing provincial and special city level officials to engage in foreign trade negotiations, the more frequent addition of end-users—that is, actual engineers—to Chinese negotiating teams, proposals for new "trade-free zones" on the Hong Kong and Macao borders, and finally extensive Chinese talk about the possibilities of compensatory trade for joint ventures.[8] The Chinese also showed interest in the possible use of credits, but only in the form of government-to-government loans and the World Bank. By the spring of 1980, China's foreign trade was growing at a reasonably steady rate, and traders continued to maintain their interest, not for

---

[8]In such compensatory trade arrangements the Chinese suggested that plants be established in China that would produce products based on the technology of the foreign partner that the foreign partner would then be expected to sell abroad. Any initial Chinese commitment of foreign exchange would be readily paid back, the foreign firms could count on cheap Chinese labor, but would have to shoulder all responsibilities for marketing the products. The arrangement is most attractive with respect to exploiting raw materials, such as oil, but of more questionable interest for consumer products involving high quality control.

the dream-world benefits they once expected, but for more mundane contracts.

This new phase of pragmatism brought with it much confusion as to precisely whom the Westerners should try to deal with. In the past the foreign traders were limited to the Canton Trade Fairs and then to the Ministry of Economic Relations with Foreign Countries, but with the new opening up it became possible to negotiate directly with any of the numerous foreign trade corporations, the ministries, and even with individual Chinese enterprises. The foreign trader now discovered that he was often talking with inappropriate Chinese officials and unable to find out exactly whom he ought to be meeting with. For many the thrill of greater access was soon replaced by the nightmare of being lost in China's mushy realm of officialdom.

By the spring of 1981 there were further reasons for taking a more sober view of the trade prospects with China. The new "reappraisal" policies were cutting more deeply than first expected. In addition to the unilateral termination of plans for a Baoshan steel mill, there were cancellations amounting to billions of dollars of contracts for a petrochemical industrial park in Nanjing, a Dangfang petrochemical complex, a Yenshan petrochemical complex in Beijing, a Xengli petrochemical industrial zone, a Giangxi copper mine, and other major developments. As the Chinese faced the dangers of inflation and anxieties over shortages of foreign exchange, they became less interested in imports and more concerned about exports, compensatory trade, joint ventures, and other means for quickly earning foreign exchange. However, despite official demands that they should be more tough-minded about buying foreign technologies, the Chinese did in fact continue to import large amounts of machinery.

As can be seen from this brief review, the problems of trade negotiations with China have not been constant; and at different periods foreigners and Chinese had different expectations and levels of optimism. It has been generally hard for Chinese and foreigners alike to share a sense of what should be taken as reality. This study will not make a point of distinguishing the negotiating styles at each phase of this history but will concentrate on more general patterns that have been more prominent during some periods than others. The goal will be to stress themes and propositions that will be useful for future negotiations with the Chinese. However, when it is appropriate, differences will be noted in Chinese negotiating practices under varying conditions, such as when it is either they or the foreign party who is the most anxious for agreement, or when they are working from strength or weakness, or any differences that seem to influence Chinese practices.

DIFFERENT TREATMENT FOR DIFFERENT TYPES OF BUYERS AND SELLERS

The Chinese obviously use different practices when negotiating with a major multinational enterprise than they use with a medium or small firm. But certain general attitudes and policies influence their negotiating styles.

First, large, highly capitalized, and usually high technology firms are seeking markets for their products or services and generally believe that what they have to offer should be very important to China's Four Modernizations. Such firms usually believe that they should be of great interest to the Chinese, that what they offer are self-evidently priority matters, and therefore they are natural trading partners with the Chinese. At the same time, however, these firms tend to have intense competitors and aggressive sales practices. They are usually rich enough so that Chinese stalling tactics are irritating but not defeating. The Chinese are interested in what they have to offer, and hope to learn much from them, but they also are extremely cautious in actually buying from them. They would rather learn their technologies than buy their products. This kind of company provided most of the Hong Kong and Japanese respondents for this study.

The second category of companies is in China to buy raw materials. They are usually a part of China's traditional foreign trade system. Because they are usually buying standardized raw materials for which there are other suppliers in the world market, there is little complexity in their negotiations with the Chinese. It is through such companies that the Chinese carry out the major portion of their foreign trade. Aside from the Japanese trading companies, who have interest in such buying, not many representatives of such companies were interviewed. Those who were uniformly gave the Chinese high marks and few criticisms for their practices.

The third type of firm is interested in importing consumer items from China, for example handicrafts and clothing. Because of their need to be extremely sensitive to fashions, fads, and consumer tastes they often have to engage in hard bargaining with the Chinese to ensure that the Chinese deliver what is wanted. What they buy is not a significant portion of China's exports, but because the items have high visibility, the Chinese have a prestige interest in the negotiations.

Finally, there are firms that seek to set up production facilities in China in the hopes of lowering their costs. The Chinese generally have a great interest in such companies for they hope to reap quick foreign exchange rewards, provide jobs, and transfer appropriate technologies. These companies must be exceptionally careful in their negotiations because they seek more than just payments or products from the Chinese. Fortunately, the complexity of their negotiations is somewhat counterbalanced by the enthusiasm of the Chinese for any prospects of joint venture or compensatory trade.

THE GENERAL SOURCES OF DIFFICULTY

Before dealing with the more specific problems in negotiations with the Chinese, we need to recognize that in the most general terms there have been three principal sources of difficulty: (1) problems that arise from the newness of the relations and the lack of experience on both sides; (2) problems inherent in capitalist enterprises seeking to do business with a centrally planned, socialist economy; and (3) cultural characteristics of both Chinese and Americans.

Problems of Novelty

A large proportion of the specific problems that have plagued the negotiations between American businessmen and Chinese officials can be attributed to the newness of the relations and the lack of precedence and experience on both sides. Both Chinese and Americans have been going through a learning experience, and naturally there have been misunderstandings. Presumably, most of these difficulties will be of short duration and should decline with time and practice, and it is hoped they will not be so serious as to leave any permanent damage to the overall relationship between the two countries.

The problems of novelty have had a wide range and were more acute during the first two phases of China's opening. Many of the problems were of a housekeeping nature, as for example when the Chinese negotiating schedules bore no relationship to the period allotted for hotel reservations. Others involved the complexities of the Chinese government and the uncertainties created for Americans when one set of Chinese officials would say "yes" and another "no." More basic were confusions over how seriously one was to treat signed letters of intent or protocols. Many problems remain as each side finds it difficult to learn the ways of the other. Americans find it impossible to believe that the Chinese system is inherently incapable of giving decisive up or down decisions in a short time span. Chinese have equal difficulty in appreciating that American firms cannot give China unlimited time or that there should be a relationship between the monetary value of a contract and the amount of time devoted to negotiating it.

Some of the larger and more responsible American enterprises decided to wait out this confused period of learning, allowing others to run up a record of mistakes; they plan to enter the China trade only when the patterns are more clearly established. This meant that among those who pioneered were a disproportionate number of aggressive entrepreneurs, many of whom enjoyed disregarding risk. Thus, the incidence of mistakes and misunderstandings was probably greater because of both the absence of the more cautious and the abundance of the more brazen. By now those who have remained in the China trade are almost all responsible business firms, and most of the early adventurers have lost interest in China.

Although more experienced and responsible American businessmen decided to pass over the early rounds of the China opening, it has, of course, been impossible for the U.S. government to withdraw temporarily until such a learning phase could have been completed. Yet, like the private sector, the U.S. government had an early phase of exuberance during which so many segments wanted to participate in the drama of the new opening with China that both the Chinese and the American systems became overloaded and unsound decisions were taken. In retrospect, it was clearly not prudent for so many parts of the U.S. government to have engaged in negotiations so early in the new relationship. In the future, the initiating of proposals should be spaced so that the learning experience for both sides can be better absorbed. For a time in 1977-78, helping China with the Four Modernizations created false expectations among the Chinese, especially about the willingness of the United States to provide substantial assistance.

The problems of novelty have been great not only because of the prolonged period of separation of the two countries, but also because the dramatic opening of China quickly generated exaggerated expectations on all sides about how much trade was likely to take place. In the first year after the ouster of the Gang of Four, the Chinese grossly overstated the pace at which their planned modernization would proceed. Chinese officials were also completely unaware of how far their procedures deviated from standard international practices and therefore how much they had to learn.

American businessmen initially had even more unrealistic expectations. Although most were aware that there was much to learn about the mechanics of doing business with the Chinese, they were largely naive about the rhetoric of China's modernization. Almost to a man, American businessmen entered China trade with the idea that the Chinese were in a great hurry to catch up with the world, and therefore anyone who wished to be their partner would have to step lively and promise quick action. Only after much frustration and confusion did they learn that the Chinese were content to move at a sedate pace.

The vast majority of our American informants said that a most difficult thing they had to learn about doing business with China was to disregard Chinese heroic rhetoric about catching up and to adopt the guiding principle of *patience*. They said repeatedly the ultimate secret of successful negotiations with the Chinese was to repress any urge to hurry the process along. Although they belong to a culture that accepts the exaggerations of political campaign rhetoric, American businessmen have not always appreciated that Chinese leaders also find it politically useful to confuse hope and reality. It has been especially disconcerting to these Americans that the Chinese feel no need even to modify their budgetary priorities to conform to their proclaimed promises.[9] Later we shall return to problems that come from cultural differences between Americans and Chinese about the relationship of symbol and reality, between rhetoric and actual intentions, and the concept of hypocrisy.

The difficulty of learning patience in dealing with China has been compounded not only by Chinese rhetoric and American excitement over new opportunities promised by China's opening, but also by the period of uncertainty that American businessmen must usually go through before they learn even whether they will have the opportunity to compete in the China market. The wait as the Chinese slowly respond to initial letters of inquiry produces an anxious state of anticipation, especially when it is public knowledge that one's competitors are already in Beijing. Then there is the anxiety over whether or when the visa will be issued for the chief executive officer to make the first visit to China. Finally, when the Americans at last arrive in Beijing fully primed for action with their sales speeches and engineering demonstrations, comes the shock of learning that the Chinese are in no hurry.

One of our respondents described the shock and frustration:

> You have been waiting months to hear from the Chinese; then when you do, a whole team goes to work helping to prepare your presentation. When you arrive at the hotel, full of anticipation, your Chinese contact says, "How about visiting the Great Wall tomorrow?" So you agree, but then the next day it is the Ming Tombs, then the Forbidden City, the Temple of Heaven, and so on. You came to do business

---

[9]The resistance to change in budget priorities among Chinese leaders was recently documented when Fox Butterfield showed that in spite of Science and Technology being one of the Four Modernizations, and in spite of the tremendous new emphasis upon academically competitive examinations for college admission, the Chinese still allocate only 1.1 percent of gross national income to education, just as they have done since the early 1960s (*New York Times,* July 13, 1980).

and you expected them to be in a big hurry, and it turns out that they would rather spend time leisurely sightseeing and chatting.

Many respondents are convinced that the Chinese consciously use such slowdown techniques as bargaining ploys because they believe they can exploit a natural American tendency for impatience. Whether conscious or not, the practice of slowdown is made much more effective by the Americans' false expectations that the Chinese are working under the pressure of time.

When an official of a Japanese trading firm was asked whether the Japanese had experienced similar misunderstandings about the urgency of China's modernization plans, he replied:

> We Japanese have known the Chinese for a long, long time. We got our written characters from them, our Buddhist religion, and, of course, we also came to know them very well because of what our militarists did. On the basis of this long and intimate acquaintance we know very well that the Chinese are not going to modernize very fast.

The public record, however, suggests that at one time Japanese businessmen were just as impatient as the Americans later became and that both are having to learn from experience how to adapt to Chinese ways.

Problems in Mating a Communist and a Capitalist System

The second general category of early problems in negotiations between Americans and Chinese involves the more long-range difficulties inherent in business dealings between a socialist, centrally planned, command economy and a competitive, pluralistic, capitalistic system. Awareness that Deng Xiaoping's China is different from Mao's China has caused many American businessmen to assume, falsely, that China is on the verge of abandoning communism and becoming much like the other East Asian countries. On one side of the table sit state negotiators who must be sensitive to issues of national pride and national interest, to currents in political ideology, and, above all, to the politics of state planning and bureaucratic allocations; on the other side are private negotiators who can swallow pride, scorn politics and ideology, and need only the calculation of profit to guide them. Bureaucratic rigidities cannot bend easily to the desires for spontaneity and special consideration of private American companies. Structurally, there is a lack of symmetry as a multiplicity of autonomous American entrepreneurs compete with each other in dealing with a bureaucratic hierarchy that is supposedly monolithic but in practice is not well integrated.

Ironically, one of the main considerations causing American businessmen to forget that China is still a socialist system is also one of the problems of novelty just mentioned—the uncertainty over precisely whom they should be trying to do business with. Multiple contacts suggest a pluralistic system rather than a rigid state-controlled one. In dealing with the Soviet Union and with Eastern European socialist countries, American companies are confronted with a well-defined bureaucratic structure in which it is fairly easy to determine who would be responsible for any particular matter of business. In the case of the Soviet Union, the foreign trade "system" begins with the Ministry of Foreign Trade, which is directly under the State Council and has under it some 60 foreign trade organizations with specialized responsibilities.[10] Negotiations are usually divided between a first-stage technical phase and then a clearly separate commercial or financial phase in which the terms and conditions of the transaction are negotiated.[11] Although, as Marshall Goldman has warned, doing business with the Soviets "means extra time, money, and ulcers,"[12] the initial contacts are more orderly than in China trade. According to tables of organization, the Chinese appear somewhat to follow the Soviet bureaucratic model, but in practice since 1979, the Chinese system is less clearly structured, leading to initial confusion but also the promise of greater flexibility.

The Chinese also have a Ministry of Foreign Trade, but under it is the key China Council for the Promotion of International Trade, with its changing numbers of subordinate sub-councils. Parallel to the Council and also under the Ministry of Foreign Trade are ten specialized Import-Export corporations, where most traders start their search for Chinese partners.[13] In addition, it is possible to negotiate directly with the state institutions actually responsible for various technologies and enterprises. Finally, the Chinese have also opened the door to direct negotiations with provincial and special city officials, a degree of apparent decentralization that much to the pleasure of many American traders often brings them into direct contact with the end users of what they are trying to sell. In actual

---

[10]John W. DePauw, *Soviet American Trade Negotiations,* Praeger, New York, 1979, Chapter 2.

[11]*Ibid.,* p. 43.

[12]Marshall I. Goldman, *Detente and Dollars: Doing Business with the Soviets,* Basic Books, New York, 1975, p. 153, quoted in DePauw, p. 9.

[13]For China's current organization of foreign trade, see Tom Gorman and Jeffrey S. Muir, *Advertising in the People's Republic of China,* China Consultants International, Hong Kong, Ltd., 1979, pp. 82-83.

fact, however, the Chinese system is still highly centralized in that any significant allocation of foreign exchange is controlled by the Bank of China, which must review most contract negotiations.[14]

Most American businessmen welcome the complexity and to some degree greater flexibility of the Chinese system for it suggests that they are not confronted with as rigid a bureaucracy as in the Soviet Union.[15] However, the situation also causes frustration as traders feel uncertain whether they are actually talking with the right organization or wasting their time. Traders keep asking themselves whether it is better to be dealing directly with, say, the Third Machine Ministry or with the Chinese National Machinery Corporation headquarters in Beijing, or with the actual factory in Shenyang—unsure of where they should be, they suspect that their competitors have found the right entry point. Because the Chinese bureaucracy is not well coordinated horizontally, it is usually impossible to obtain guidance from middle level cadres about other possible interested parties. Officials are usually knowledgeable only about activities within their own cellular hierarchy and are completely ignorant about parallel hierarchies. Indeed, several veteran American businessmen have had Chinese officials ask them about practices in other Chinese ministries, suggesting that even fairly high Chinese officials assume that foreign businessmen have greater opportunities to learn about parallel bureaucracies than they have.

Frustration over uncertainty about the right office to negotiate with is compounded by the overwhelming surface evidence that China is an exceptionally well-ordered authoritarian society, which makes the individual businessman believe more than ever that somewhere in the confusing world of Chinese officialdom there must be someone who is in charge of precisely the matter that concerns him. The American keeps asking, "How can a society be so well organized in all manner of little matters and be so mushy and indecisive when it comes to the important matter of organizing for foreign trade?"

This problem brings us to the larger issue of American lack of understanding of the nature of authority in China, which will play an

---

[14]For an excellent brief review of China's organization for foreign trade before the 1979 increases in potential contact points, see Christopher Howe, *China's Economy: A Basic Guide,* Basic Books, New York, 1978, pp. 129-150.

[15]During the fall of 1980 the Chinese press carried numerous articles in praise of the market mechanism, but then on December 2 the *People's Daily* published a major editorial, reflecting in all probability a Politburo decision, stating that central planning must be basic.

[16]For a discussion of the lack of horizontal communications within the Chinese bureaucracy, see A. Doak Barnett, *Cadres, Bureaucracy and Political Power in Communist China,* Columbia University Press, New York, 1967.

important part in the analysis. Americans assume that power and responsibility should be clearly related, that there should be somebody in charge of any important activity, and that if that person makes a decision then everything should follow accordingly. Moreover, the more authoritarian the system the quicker subordinates have to comply with the wishes of the one in charge. In contrast the Chinese system, while undeniably authoritarian, is in its essence a bureaucratic process in which the critical art is to avoid responsibilities, diffuse decisions, and blunt all commands that might later leave one vulnerable to criticisms.[17] In short, there is usually no particular person in command who can cut through problems and procedures and produce effective command decisions in the way Americans fancy it to be possible.

Americans in both the private and public sectors persist in trying to find a particular person who has command authority at each level of the Chinese system. In Chinese political culture there is no assumption that power must be tied to responsibility; on the contrary, in the ranks of the powerful, proof of importance lies precisely in being shielded from accountability. All high officials like to convey the aura of omnipotence, but they also expect that those below them will protect them from criticism; and this means, above all, protecting them from their own mistakes.[18]

The American belief that executive authority should, and usually does, take on czar-like, or maybe more appropriately emperor-like, command can be seen in American expectations about Deng Xiaoping's growing powers. American government officials hope that Vice Premier Deng will become the absolute master of all of China, and many American businessmen have come to believe that if only he were the unambiguous top leader of China then all their problems of dealing with confused authorities would evaporate.

Chief executives of two major American corporations greatly em-

---

[17]On Chinese bureaucratic skills in diffusing responsibilities, see Lucian W. Pye, *The Dynamics of Factions and Consensus in Chinese Politics: A Model and Some Propositions,* The Rand Corporation, R-2566-AF, July 1980.

[18]There is a strange paradox in these conflicting views in that they seem to contradict what might at first be expected of each political culture. In American political culture it is common to assume that authority is both limited and divided, and therefore it is paradoxical that Americans tend to want to find strong men in foreign countries, be it the Shah in Iran or Deng Xiaoping in Beijing. In contrast, in Chinese political culture the conventional pretense is that authority is omnipotent and that it is improper to seek to define the limits of authority with any precision. In practice, this pretense about authority is maintained by the skill with which leaders avoid demonstrating where the limits of their authority might in fact be. Thus, all of those at the "Center" act as though they have complete authority, carefully avoiding situations in which their powers are visibly circumscribed. Once the authority of any one of the leaders is manifestly checked, it is quickly assumed that he is about to lose all power.

barrassed their firms because they innocently assumed that when the presumably most powerful administrative decisionmaker in Beijing personally informed them that China would go ahead with their proposals, it meant that a deal had been made. Subsequently, when the Chinese failed to follow up with detailed contracts, it was broadly assumed that the Americans had been premature in announcing their expected accomplishments and that they were thus naive. The Americans were, in fact, naive, not because of misunderstanding what had been said, but because they assumed that the "top man's" words would prevail. Their problem, like that of so many other businessmen, was that they believed China was an effectively functioning authoritarian system in which the wishes of leaders become the law, especially as there is no other source for laws except the will of the leaders.

Failure to understand the nature of Chinese bureaucratic authority has also made it difficult for the traders to understand the causes of the hyper-cautious attitudes and endless suspicions of Chinese cadres. Most businessmen do not appreciate that all Chinese officials must carefully protect themselves against all possible criticisms, including what might happen if policies were to change. Hence, at all times Chinese officials have to practice the bureaucratic art of "covering their tails," in the American vernacular.

Unwilling to believe that the officials they were dealing with could lack self-confidence and autonomy, some of the interviewed American businessmen reported that they had first assumed that the Chinese were only manifesting the consequences of a hundred years of earlier exploitation by Westerners when they were suspicious of the motives of foreign traders. Working with such a hypothesis, they sought to gain the confidence of those who apparently distrusted them by stressing that their firms were new and hence untainted by any of the practices associated with the earlier era. That only made the Chinese officials more cautious and suspicious because they now might be vulnerable to the criticism of dealing with unsubstantial and untried foreign firms. The Americans reported they realized their mistake when they saw the Chinese had obvious preferences for dealing with the old British trading firms, such as Jardines, which are synonymous with Treaty Port China.

The universal fear within the Chinese bureaucracy of being charged with not upholding China's national interests contributes to making Chinese negotiators exceptionally meticulous, astute, and tough, people who have extraordinary endurance and the ability to negotiate seemingly forever. Attempts to resolve differences that might be readily resolved with others at the bargaining table will in the Chinese case have to be referred to superiors, hence be the occasion for prolonged delays. From the Chinese point of view such circumstances are not causes for embarrassment because they will probably increase the level of frustration of the foreign negotiators and make them more ready in the future to suppress objections.

Even in government-to-government negotiations about commercial matters, U.S. officials find themselves at a disadvantage because of the socialist nature of the Chinese system. For example, when Boyd Hight, the chief U.S. negotiator of the first air agreement between the United States and the PRC, had to admit failure in achieving the standard American requirement of two competing American airlines on any international route, he said, "I don't see how you can get the sort of agreement we usually want when you are dealing with a country with a controlled economy."[19]

American problems of understanding socialist China are to a lesser degree matched by Chinese misconceptions about capitalistic American practices. Several businessmen reported that the Chinese they were dealing with could not believe that the American companies could be as uncoordinated and autonomous in their actions as they claimed to be. Their Marxist theories about "Wall Street" and "monopoly capitalism" had convinced them that behind the helter-skelter, uncoordinated, and contradictory activities of the competing Americans there had to be a hidden design. Similarly, they often revealed their conviction that the U.S. government and the businessmen had to be working more closely with each other than in fact was the case, for after all, were they not both the servants of "Wall Street"?

Thus, there is a strange, but understandable, problem of false perceptions by both sides: The Chinese assume that the Americans are more coordinated in their actions and more centrally controlled by Washington than in fact is the case, and the Americans remain confused about the extent to which China differs from their picture of a socialist, centrally controlled society; and in spite of their search for a czar-like authority in each realm, they continue to treat China as being more pluralistic than in fact it is.

In the actual negotiating processes Americans and Chinese act in ways that contradict each one's false preconceptions of the other. The effect is raised suspicion and distrust. American negotiators are puzzled and upset when the Chinese negotiators they have pictured as pragmatic, profit-oriented managers of specific enterprises suddenly introduce nationalistic considerations into the deliberations or display an overriding sensitivity to the dictates of higher authorities at the "Center." The Americans suspect that the Chinese, in reverting to

---

[19]Jay Mathews, *Washington Post*, September 9, 1980.

expected communist form, must only be engaging in tactical ploys. Because the Americans did not want to believe that the Chinese still have as centralized an economy as they necessarily must, they therefore wonder whether the friendly cadres with whom they had been working could be engaging in some form of stalling tactic.

On the other side, the Chinese frequently become suspicious of Americans who go to inordinate lengths to communicate their autonomy from the U.S. government and indicate that they have only personal motives for wanting to help China modernize. As Leites has noted in analyzing U.S.-Soviet arms control negotiations, a characteristic American assumption is that one can convince the other party of one's trustworthiness and objectivity by suggesting that in spite of being an official one is somehow distant from political power.[20] Soviet negotiators, in contrast, and also apparently the Chinese, are anxious to exaggerate the extent to which they speak for ultimate authority. Iklé has also noted this American propensity to seek a "mediator's" role in negotiations, and he has wondered, "If American officials mediate between the United States and the Soviet position, while Russian officials defend the position of their government as final, who is left to defend the U.S. position?"[21]

The businessmen I interviewed manifested to an exceptionally high degree this American trait of wanting to be mediators. Not only did they understandably make a point of suggesting disagreement with official American policies if they felt that such policies might be offensive to the Chinese, but even when no issues existed they still believed they were creating a good impression with the Chinese by disassociating themselves from the values of the American government and of American national policies. Several of the Americans explicitly said that they believed they were proving their sincerity with the Chinese by their unsolicited criticism of past and even present U.S. policies. Yet the Chinese must question the "sincerity" of people who make a show of not visiting the American Embassy in Beijing while representing firms and banks singled out in Communist literature as among those that control Washington and the entire American system.

None of the Japanese businessmen believed there are advantages in seeming to be far removed from the center of power in Japan. Indeed, even before normalization, when the Japanese companies negotiated annual trade agreements with the Chinese, they leaned in the direction of making their agreements appear as "official" as possible. Al-

---

[20]Nathan Leites, *Styles in Negotiations: East and West on Arms Control, 1958-1961,* The Rand Corporation, RM-2838-ARPA, November 1961, pp. 245-249.

[21]Iklé (1967), p. 149.

though there are other difficulties in Sino-Japanese negotiations, the Chinese probably find the more explicit and openly acknowledged relations between business and government in Japan to be a more plausible, hence a more honest system than the complete separation of business and government that the American businessmen virtuously idealize.

Although the Chinese have made great strides in suppressing ideological issues and Americans are extremely anxious to put aside past polemics, both Chinese and Americans find it hard to understand each others' political and economic systems, which brings us to the larger issue of cultural misunderstandings.

CULTURAL FACTORS

Unquestionably the largest and possibly the most intractable category of problems in Sino-American business negotiations can be traced to the cultural differences between the two societies. Inevitably, frustrations and misunderstandings arise in the meeting of representatives from two such different cultures as China and America. For example, the Chinese concept of friendship and more specifically their expectations of what friends should be willing to do for each other goes well beyond American notions of friendliness. Consequently the building of "friendly" relationships in the negotiations process can lead to exaggerated expectations of dependency that, if not satisfied, can cause angry reactions and feelings of having been mistreated.

It is not really possible to isolate culture as a separate category because it influences all actions. Cultural factors affect the process of learning about each other and color China's state planning practices and the spirit of American enterprise. Furthermore, cultural factors will surface throughout the remainder of this study.

That being the case, only two general problems deserve special attention because they are so frequently identified in discussions of Sino-American cultural differences. The first is that Chinese culture traditionally shuns legal considerations and instead stresses ethical and moralist principles, whereas Americans are thought to be highly legalistic. The second is the difference between the all-pervasive influence of politics in Chinese Communist culture and the American view that politics, economics, and social relations occupy separate spheres. Incompatible views about the law, particularly as applied to contracts, and about the possibility of separating politics from other aspects of life could produce very disturbing consequences for smooth negotiations.

Historically, the great clash between Chinese and Western cultures revolved around quite different views about the importance of legal processes, and the result, of course, was the Western imposition upon China of the Treaty Port System and what the Chinese came to call the "Unequal Treaties."[22] Today Americans seeking to do business with China have some of the same problems that troubled European traders in the mid-19th century. China still does not have an institutionalized legal system, and Beijing is still developing a commercial code that would govern joint ventures and other forms of contractual relationships.

American traders today do not seem to be as troubled by the cavalier Chinese view of legal procedures as were their 19th century predecessors. Many of the businessmen interviewed told of how they had learned that among Chinese it was the traditional custom to seal agreements with only an oral commitment, a nod of the head, or a handshake. In short, the Americans have generally been willing to be flexible and adapt to what they understand to be the nonlegalistic ways of the Chinese.

In the first encounters the Chinese usually seem to be bound by their traditional nonlegalistic practices. The first objective of Chinese negotiators is usually to get an agreement on general principles about the character of the evolving relationship. The agreement is only an objective and the general form of the relationship, with little attention to details. Most American legal departments find such initial contacts very troublesome precisely because they seem to leave out all the particulars expected in a signed legal document. The Chinese usually insist at the initial stage that the details can be worked out later as long as both sides take a positive attitude toward the spirit of the general principles.

To this extent, problems arise because of the Chinese view of legal processes. But it would be quite wrong to assume that the Chinese are entirely uninformed about Western legal practices. It is true that they start negotiations in a very unlegalistic manner, but their goal is almost always to arrive at carefully worded contracts. Numerous cases were described in which the Chinese were quick to exploit legalisms if they could be turned to China's advantage.

One amusing case was that of an American firm seeking to sell China a new form of pesticide. It prepared to offer a free sample to test the product's efficacy in the Chinese environment. The Chinese officials insisted that China would have to pay something for the sample

---

[22]John K. Fairbank, *The United States and China,* Harvard University Press, Cambridge, 1971, pp. 105-149.

because it was against the principles of the Chinese people to accept charity. The American tried to explain that it was his company's standard practice to allow potential customers to try out products at no expense, but the Chinese officials were firm in saying that they would take nothing free. Puzzled as to what to do, the American finally suggested a token payment, but he also made it clear that the actual price would, of course, be much higher. A year later when the Chinese decided the product indeed had merit, a new Chinese negotiating team sought to make substantial purchases. To the American's dismay they insisted that the price would have to be "last year's, plus allowances for inflation." The new team rejected the American's protest that the previous "sale" was only symbolic, based on a nominal price because it was really a free sample, because the documents did not show that to have been the case, and they could not admit to their superiors that the previous year's team could get a better price.

Whatever may be the influences of traditional Chinese culture on law, cadres now engaged in negotiations have learned that records are critical in determining career advancements. They appreciate the significance of written reports and legalistic documentation, yet realize that they can be protected when something is not included in the written record. In short, most Chinese officials are well aware of the advantages of avoiding precise written commitments as to their part of an agreement, and of inserting precise commitments for the foreigner—an attitude that does not make them too different from good American negotiators. Probably, because they need to protect themselves bureaucratically, the Chinese try for more crudely advantageous deals, while American businessmen are more willing to be evenhanded, spelling out in equal detail (or with equal vagueness) the obligations of both parties.[23]

In sum, the situation seems to be that both the Americans and the Chinese understand the other's attitude toward law and legal procedures, but each is prepared to adjust only to his own advantage. Neither is completely at ease with the other's practices. Therefore, although the crude cultural misunderstandings of the 19th century no longer apply, a residue of potential misunderstanding remains, espe-

---

[23]There are, however, many examples of the Chinese displaying high legal skills, even to the point of benefiting the foreign party. For example, after Siemens had concluded a contract with the China National Machinery Import Corporation that satisfied its lawyers in Germany, the Chinese legal experts at the parent China Council for the Promotion of International Trade, on reviewing the contract, found many flaws and ambiguities, several of which might have damaged Siemens's interests. The Chinese insisted that a new contract, drafted by their legal specialists, replace the one Siemens had already signed.

cially because each side fancies that it has leaned over backward to play the game according to the other's rules.

Can politics be separated from business? Again, both Chinese and Americans apparently understand that the two cultures differ on this question: The Chinese view, both traditional and Communist, is that politics is all-pervasive; Americans believe they can separate politics from business. In actual practice, each side tries to react in terms of what it thinks is the national predisposition of the other, and thus a reversal of roles takes place. Many American businessmen, especially during the early phase of dealings with the Chinese, say that they sought to gain favor with the Chinese by manifesting political awareness. In some cases, the effort involved high company policy, such as dramatically ending operations in Taiwan; more frequently, the attempts to curry favor take the form of expressing enthusiasm for revolutionary precepts and Chinese theater and art. Anecdotes abound about American businessmen espousing Maoist themes even after the fall of the Gang of Four and thereby irritating their Chinese hosts.

In contrast to this uncharacteristic American eagerness to introduce political notes into business relationships, Chinese officials currently responsible for commercial activities are usually starkly apolitical, concentrating on purely business and technical matters. This was not the case during the first years after the Shanghai Communique, which may explain why many businessmen have felt that they had to be politically partisan if they were to have success with the Chinese. Long after the Chinese have become "pragmatic," however, many American businessmen still feel that it is appropriate to introduce political views into the negotiating process, whereas the Chinese have no problem in becoming completely businesslike.

These two examples of reversals in what have been assumed to be cultural concepts suggest the subtlety with which cultural factors must be analyzed in the negotiating process. When both sides are consciously trying to hit upon winning tactics, each will know something about the presumed cultural characteristics of the other and each will adjust his behavior accordingly. The act of consciously trying to adhere to the standards of the other creates a sense of credit due. Each feels consciously or unconsciously that the other party should appreciate the deference that has been shown to its cultural ways. Each party expects some rewards for acting in an unnatural way, and each can build some feelings of resentment for the failure of the other to show appreciation.

The conscious efforts to take into account the other party's cultural practices can eliminate certain gross misunderstandings, but cultural factors continue to surface and cause problems in more subtle and indirect ways.

II. THE AMBIENCE OF NEGOTIATIONS

Certain historical, structural, and even geographical factors characterize both private and public negotiations with the Chinese and give them certain inherent advantages. The Chinese do not necessarily seek these advantages, and indeed the Americans often contribute to their existence either by a lack of foresight (or concern) or because they accept the idea that there should be some form of payment for merely the opportunity to do business with the Chinese.

Even before substantive discussions take place, the stage is usually set in ways that affect the negotiating styles of the two sides. In particular, the ambience of the occasion casts the Americans as anxious supplicants and the Chinese as passive and somewhat relaxed hosts.

THE COSTS AND BENEFITS OF BRINGING OUT THE BIG GUNS FIRST

To an amazing extent, negotiations by American companies with the Chinese have followed the pattern of the U.S. government negotiations with Beijing, in which Americans enthusiastically violate one of the first principles of negotiations and diplomacy—namely, that summit meetings should never take place without extensive preliminary spade work by subordinate officials.[1] In the American business world (as in conventional diplomacy), chief executive officers of companies (or heads of state and foreign ministers) properly insist that their subordinates work out as far as possible all the negotiating details before they enter the last stage of the process to resolve any remaining problems and to consummate the agreement. In the case of negotiations with the Chinese the reverse has been the standard practice. Chief executive officers and board chairmen insist that they themselves should be first to visit China and open negotiations with the Chinese. The impetus for such behavior is, of course, the status symbol associated with visiting China—the "Westchester County Syndrome," which is characterized by the boast that "I have just been to China" and "I opened the way for our company to do business with the PRC."

Dr. Henry Kissinger and President Richard Nixon, in opening rela-

---

[1]Sir Harold Nicolson, *Diplomacy,* Harcourt, Brace, New York, 1939; Charles W. Thayer, *Diplomat,* Harper and Brothers, New York, 1959; Dean Rusk, "The President," *Foreign Affairs,* XXXVIII, No. 3, April 1960.

tions with China, personally conducted the preliminary round of negotiations, proclaiming that they had been highly successful in reaching understandings with the Chinese; only later did they assign subordinate officials to take over the tasks of negotiating substantive issues.[2] A surprisingly large number of American corporations have followed the same pattern.

After their first encounters with the Chinese, chief executive officers return to report that they were outstandingly successful and that they found the Chinese to be most cooperative and easy people with whom to do business. The middle-level executive who follows to work out the details comes under great pressure. He is reluctant to indicate that he is less skillful in negotiating than his superiors; and, of course, he must feel constrained not to act in ways that might irritate the Chinese and spoil the relationship established by his boss. Consequently, all subsequent and substantive negotiations for the American side need to be especially careful to avoid offending the Chinese. Most American negotiators, from both private companies and the U.S. government, seem to feel that relations with China were excellent when they entered the scene and that they might be held responsible if these relations should deteriorate.

When the top business executives are sent first into the field, the American companies lose the advantage of dispatching their highest officials for critical negotiations at a point of consummation. Having brought in the "big guns" at the beginning, any second appearance of the American principal must be limited to a meeting on generalities at which civilities prevail, and when it would be extremely awkward to argue over details, to say nothing of applying pressure on the Chinese.

The middle-level executive assigned to do the substantive negotiations is soon under considerable pressure. As one of them explained:

> The president and the chairman of the board both went home from Beijing as instant authorities on China, and ever since they have assumed that they are completely knowledgeable about how to do business with the Chinese. With respect to any other part of the world they defer to the specialized knowledge of the man in the field, but not on China. When I report problems in the negotiations, I sense that they are impatient with me rather than with the Chinese. They have no sense of how stubborn the Chinese can be over terms. Their memories are filled with enjoyable encounters with the Chinese

---

[2]Henry Kissinger writes in his memoirs that President Nixon manifestly wanted to be the first to visit China, even suggesting that Kissinger might meet with the Chinese outside of China and if that was not possible then maybe the announcement of the meeting should not mention the names of the officials involved. Henry Kissinger, *The White House Years,* Little, Brown and Co., Boston, 1979, pp. 734-735.

when all the talk was about how good it was going to be working together. When I try to report problems to the home office, their first reaction is always that I must be the cause of the difficulties; that it is my fault that I have not got the hang of how to have agreeable relations with the Chinese. The truth is that at every turn I have to bend over backward not to offend the Chinese. I have to keep my side of the record perfect or I'll be criticized by New York or by the Chinese or by both. Above all I cannot call upon my boss to step in and back me up at key points in the negotiations. He wants to come back out for another visit, but only after everything is in order.

Apparently many American companies are not troubled by these pragmatic problems because they are more interested in the public relations payoff of being in the forefront of the China opening than in serious negotiations. Stockholders seemingly believe that management is on its toes if the chief executive officer himself has tested the China market. The Chinese have willingly cooperated in furthering such public relations gestures because they feel that China benefits from the impression that there is an endless stream of business leaders knocking on China's door.

Some American enterprises believe that there are advertising advantages in merely having a Beijing office address even if they are not able to do much business with China. Again the Chinese have not been averse to such practices, but in July 1980 they sharply raised rents for foreigners, and in September of the same year they introduced income tax laws that would make it very costly for foreign businessmen to stay in China without profitable activities.

The hazards of having to bring out the "big guns" first often cannot be avoided because the Chinese expect that senior officials should visit them. The pitfalls in having to do business in this manner can be minimized if American officers clearly recognize that the Chinese usually want only a highly generalized agreement out of such visits that in principle a relationship is possible. It is usually the Americans who feel that something more concrete must be "accomplished" to make the trip appear fruitful.

This difference in perceptions of what is to be expected from the initial meetings of the principal figures is further exaggerated by a basic difference in negotiating approaches: The Chinese insist on beginning with an agreement on general principles while the American instinct is usually to proceed from concrete matters, avoiding as much as possible conflicts over "mere rhetoric." Whereas the Chinese will subsequently exploit to their advantage the need to "adhere to agreed principles," they will also tolerate very loosely formulated initial agreements. Therefore, chief executive officers need only open the door with their initial agreement; and they should not include anything concrete with respect to time, amounts, or sums of money, or anything that will constrain their subordinates in subsequent negotiations.

The difficulties Americans have in resisting the temptation to go beyond generalities on even first meetings can be seen in the way they work to make every official visit to Beijing the occasion for a newsworthy agreement on some substantive matter. Apparently American officials believe that the relationship with China can be advanced only if there are detailed agreements whenever principals meet. In contrast, whenever high Chinese officials travel abroad they rarely seek agreements on specific matters, only on symbolic generalities.

THE HOME COURT ADVANTAGE

A second closely related factor in the ambience of negotiations is that the Americans must follow the historical practice of being the foreigner who comes as a guest seeking permission to be allowed to do business in China. Even before the days of the Macartney and Amherst missions, the Chinese appreciated the negotiating advantages of reminding "visitors from afar" that they were the guests and that as hosts the Chinese should call the tune on procedures and the timing of meetings.[3]

This particular Chinese advantage is usually established well before the American gets to China. During the long and uncertain wait between the initial communication probes and the granting of a visa, the American businessman comes to appreciate the fact that he will be able to operate only at the tolerance of the Chinese and that it will be very easy for him to do the wrong thing once he gets to China. Indeed, the combined mysteries of Cathay and its strange version of communism suggest that it may be very hard to do the right thing in China.

Ironically for some of the businessmen, the seminars and workshops organized to help Americans do business with China increased their sense of insecurity, convincing them that only those who "know" the Chinese can be successful and that any gaffe can cause disaster. According to one respondent,

[3]The classic statement of traditional Chinese views about treating foreign "barbarians" and problems that arose in the confrontation of Western international law and Chinese concepts of suzerainty and tribute missions to China is to be found in H. B. Morse, *The International Relations of the Chinese Empire*, Longmans Green, London and New York, 3 vols., 1910-18.

> I know that the professors and government officials were trying to be helpful, but by the time we were through listening to them I was worried as to whether I could ever learn how to operate in China. When I finally got to Beijing, I was in a state in which I was just putty in the hands of my hosts, afraid to express any views for fear that I would make a mistake.

As hosts the Chinese are in a position to control not only the agenda but the pace of negotiations. The graciousness and the bountifulness of Chinese hospitality also makes it awkward to be too businesslike in starting negotiations. Indeed, this relationship of guests to hosts has several distinct consequences for the subsequent negotiations.

First, it tends to exacerbate the problem of American impatience and Chinese patience. The impatient American is made to feel even more anxious. For many this leads to an almost compulsive need to impress their hosts, perhaps compulsion to exaggerate what one can deliver and to tell more than needs to be told. The need to prove that one is really worthy of Chinese hospitality causes many businessmen to make unrealistic promises. Many American government officials behave in much the same way when they seem compelled to outdo themselves in suggesting what their departments or agencies can do to advance the Four Modernizations.

Second, by playing the host's role to the hilt, the Chinese gain the advantages of surprise and uncertainty in agenda arrangements. Even official and semi-official delegations are routinely kept completely in the dark as to schedule and agenda until after their arrival in China, which clearly communicates who is in charge. Uncertainty about the precise programming of their sales presentations has frequently thrown American businessmen off balance and left them confused as to how they should best plan their negotiating tactics. The unexpected opportunity to meet a high official, for example, can elicit a premature revealing of aspects of technology or subtle pressures to respond to Chinese blandishments. As one respondent explained:

> Even after we arrived we were not given a definite schedule. We knew we were expected to give a technical presentation and we had worked out a good one-hour briefing with charts and pictures, but they did not make it clear when that should take place, and before we knew it we had touched on most of the material in the briefing in casual conversation or in meetings with various officials. By the time they arranged for our formal presentation we had pretty well said everything, but in a very disorganized way. By the time we showed our hand at the seminar session, the Chinese were well prepared to ask pretty technical questions. In the meantime we didn't know where we stood.

Third, by playing the host's role the Chinese are able to establish recognizable standards of favoritism and play off competitors against each other. Traders quickly recognize the signs of status and learn to judge how the Chinese have decided to treat various negotiating teams. The fact that one bank or one company is given better treatment than the others can be the cause for competitive adjustments in the strategies of all the Americans concerned.

During the first years after the Shanghai Communique the Chinese usually made hotel reservations for visiting businessmen, and the types of accommodations they offered reflected their judgments about the relative status of each one. Even though the American businessmen paid their own expenses, their treatment depended less upon their expense accounts and more on the Chinese opinion of their importance. More recently, trade officials are no longer involved in hotel and other housekeeping arrangements. Indeed, the Chinese have learned a great deal about the merits of the market and of charging what the traffic will bear. Office and hotel rates for businessmen are so high now that the Chinese must be confident that they are dealing only with well-established enterprises, and foreign firms can now demonstrate to their own satisfaction their sense of self-importance. Yet, many ways remain in which the Chinese communicate favoritism, even to the point of subtly raising or lowering the businessman's status during the process of negotiation. One businessman remarked that:

> As we began to impress the Chinese more and more with the various ways in which we could assist their modernization, I was happily surprised at the ways in which they immediately began to show their appreciation. The banquets became more awesome, and we suddenly had meetings scheduled with more important officials than anyone else at the Peking Hotel.

Finally, as travelers from afar, the Americans are naturally cast in the role of supplicants asking for Chinese beneficence. The practice of asking the visitors to present technical seminars at which they explain their products further emphasizes the need of the Americans to perform in order to impress the passive Chinese. These seminars reinforce the guest-host relationship, obligating the guests to entertain the hosts in repayment for hospitality, while allowing the Chinese hosts to keep their plans and priorities quite secret. To a striking degree these seminar presentations have the quality of foreigners bringing "gifts of knowledge" to China, which are reminiscent of the times when foreigners brought tribute to impress the superior Chinese.

The Chinese do send missions abroad, but generally these delegations are not authorized to engage in concrete negotiations, their purpose being only window shopping. Such Chinese delegations generally show great interest in technologies, whetting the appetites of their American hosts and causing them to surmise that once they get a team into China, a sale should be in the offing. The Chinese, furthermore, at times tacitly cooperate in allowing foreign firms to publicize their expectations of major sales to China, thereby setting the stage for driving an even harder bargain because the foreign firms would now be embarrassed if the sale did not materialize. There seems to have been an element of this ploy in Chinese negotiations with French firms for the HOT missiles and with the British for the Harrier vertical takeoff and landing aircraft.

Although there are traveling Chinese delegations, all final decisions are made in China and foreigners must travel if they wish to make sales. The home court advantage is significant, and it does help to create an atmosphere in which the Americans seem to need the trade more than the Chinese do. There is another parallel in the public sector in that the U.S. government is constantly ahead of the Chinese in proposing measures for the modernization of China.[4]

In fairness it should be noted that a few of the businessmen found they could exploit their position as the guests for negotiating advantages. One ploy was to set the time for their departure, thereby shifting pressure onto the Chinese to schedule meetings so as to use the available time more productively. Indeed, some reported that they had had dramatic negotiating successes by threatening to break off talks and leave China for more urgent business elsewhere. This advantage clearly entailed high risks and was quite different from the basic tilt that favors the Chinese.

The overall effect of Chinese hospitality can be overwhelming, and nearly every visitor to China leaves with warm sentiments for his hosts. Yet it is significant that not all the members of Chinese host teams exude the same degree of graciousness. It can be expected that one or more members of the team will from the outset be thin-skinned about fancied slights to China and will respond abrasively. In commenting about this phenomenon, several American businessmen said that they assumed such people were the Party officials assigned to

---

[4]As hosts the Chinese now routinely expect gifts from visiting businessmen. Until 1978 it was considered gauche to present anything more than symbolic gifts to the Chinese cadres with whom one had dealings—something often bearing the company's logo. By 1980 the cadres had come to expect substantial presents. One Japanese reached new levels in gift-giving, moving up from personal articles, such as dark glasses and calculators, to color television sets. This development has caused some embarrassment for American businessmen who are not comfortable by either culture or law with giving such generous gifts.

keep an eye on what might take place. Others doubted that this was the case because they often had evidence that more senior and very hospitable officials were in fact Party members. Another theory advanced is that the Chinese consciously use a sweet and sour approach to remind the visitor that friendship is not the only theme they know and that they can be tough-minded when necessary. Whatever the reason for such contrasting behavior, the effort is apparently to make the Americans more dependent upon the friendlier persons. One businessman explained his reaction this way:

> Mr. Wu was a constant pain, and I could tell that he didn't like me. As a result I only wanted to talk with Mr. Lee and we became very friendly. I suspect that because I was uncomfortable with Mr. Wu, maybe even a bit afraid of him, I really latched onto Mr. Lee and opened up to him.

One final feature of the home court advantage for the Chinese is that many Americans find living conditions in China a severe physical strain with few creature comforts. By no means all Americans find the quality of food in China to their liking; their hotel rooms can be without air conditioning in summer and improperly heated in winter; and some 80 percent of those visiting Beijing come down with respiratory afflictions. These problems for the traveler to a quite different society contribute to making negotiations with the Chinese seem extraordinarily physically taxing. Many of our respondents commented on how tiring negotiations with the Chinese could be; and they tended to see the Chinese as absolutely tireless people, even though they do not usually work long hours.

THE SPIRIT OF FRIENDSHIP CLASHES WITH THE DESIRE FOR THE BEST

A final major element shaping the atmosphere surrounding negotiations is the constantly repeated Chinese theme of friendship. During the preliminaries to negotiations, behind their lackadaisical manner and during the leisurely sightseeing trips, the Chinese are carefully trying to read the character of the American visitors and spot their idiosyncracies. During this phase much stress is usually given to the ideal of Sino-American friendship, and indeed it can at times become the sole topic of conversation between Chinese cadres and American businessmen. The fact that the Chinese seem to have a compelling need to dwell on the subject of friendship convinced many American businessmen that reciprocity in this spirit was a prerequisite for doing business with China.

Several of our respondents report that in the early period of the opening to China, even for a while after the fall of the Gang of Four, Chinese officials often expected friendship to go beyond social conviviality and included American confessions of past mistreatment of the PRC and pledges of future concern for the interests of the regime. Yet the Chinese cadres have in recent years become increasingly skilled in suppressing whatever political enthusiasms they may have while engaged in business dealings. A residual emphasis upon friendship remains that may be more cultural than ideological. Some of the businessmen, for example, report that they found the same theme of friendship stressed in their dealings with Chinese in Hong Kong, Taiwan, and Singapore. A few even suggested that aside from the distinctive Chinese ways of manipulating friendship there is little difference on this score in doing business in China or elsewhere, because in their view all successful negotiations call for a high level of mutual trust and respect.

Some businessmen, particularly those seeking to buy consumer products from the Chinese, have successfully turned the Chinese stress on friendship to advantage. They have hosted Chinese groups in America and in the process have sought to educate them gracefully about quality standards and taste preferences in the American market. For example, Bloomingdale's, in preparation for a $10 million sale of Chinese products in its stores, brought groups of Chinese producers to America to visit their stores and learn about the American market.[5]

Directly counter to their high valuation of friendship is another Chinese trait that has become increasingly important—the Chinese craving to have only the best, regardless of the consequences. Chinese culture ranks all things hierarchically, and one should want only what is at the top. In searching out technologies and items to import, the Chinese ask what is "number one" in each line, and who is "number one" in each field. Chinese officials find it hard to believe that in highly competitive world markets there may be fluctuations in value and that standards must depend upon a wide range of tradeoff considerations.

Once the Chinese decide upon who and what is the best they show great steadfastness. Several of the businessmen told of instances of such enduring trademark loyalties. Cadres would confide to them about their abiding faith in the superiority of Parker pens, or Lucky Strike cigarettes, or Ford autos, and then confess how confused they were by the richness of contemporary consumer choices in which they

---

[5]*New York Times,* September 7, 1980, p. D1.

could not tell who makes what. Above all, they said they were vexed at the idea that a manufacturer could make products that compete with each other without any indication of which is "best."

The search for "only the best" conflicts with the concept of "friendship," and generally wins out. Numerous examples can be cited of cases in which the Chinese welcomed ideologically friendly businessmen but then abandoned them for the opportunity to deal with enterprises that could be classified as among the best.

Cultural predispositions are reinforced by cadre career considerations because Chinese officials rightly fear that they may later be criticized for not buying the best for China. Presumably a cadre would agree to contract for less than the best only if he was stupid or had been bribed, and in either case he would be punished. At one time he might have been able to defend himself by saying he had favored "a friend of China," but given the change in Chinese ideology it becomes hard to define who should be considered an old friend. For mysterious reasons, some long-time partisans of the PRC are now seen as having been associates of the discredited Gang of Four, while others remain friends in spite of all the changes. In any case, most cadres now seem to feel that prudence calls for a record of favoring the best—which in practice often means favoring the larger American multinational corporations and banks and passing over smaller enterprises.

Several of our respondents insisted that in today's political climate in China, Americans who overenthusiastically respond to ritual Chinese phrases of friendship can provoke Chinese suspicions: "They must have something to hide; otherwise why do they make so much over liking us." All of which is to say that the atmosphere for doing business with China today favors the well-established American firm that appears to understand China's needs. Companies that have terminated their operations in Taiwan to try to gain a favored position in the PRC have not necessarily won favor, and in some cases their chances may have been damaged because the Chinese have interpreted their eagerness as a sign of avarice.

Since mid-1980 there have been a few signs that the Chinese are beginning to have second thoughts about the value of the "best," particularly with respect to costly and complex technology. Some of the large turnkey operations, such as the Baoshan steel mill and the Spey airplane engine factory, have caused the Chinese to wonder whether they are capable of absorbing the most advanced technologies. Highly sophisticated methods are usually difficult to operate and maintain, and the Chinese are now able to admit to themselves that somewhat less advanced technologies may be more appropriate at this stage of development. The Chinese informed the amazed Japanese that it was probably a mistake for China to have agreed to the Baoshan plant because it incorporates the most advanced Japanese technologies; they said it would have been better to adopt American technology, which in steelmaking is a generation or so behind that of the Japanese.

The Chinese have gone through three phases: first a stress on friendship, second a concern for obtaining only the best, and now an awareness about maximum utility of the technology. Chinese pride and their determination to catch up with world standards mean that they have ruled out acquiring appropriate technologies, which they see as a sop to Third World backwardness. Because desire for friendship is not entirely dead, and the quest for the best is still strong in many quarters, cadres do find it necessary to protect themselves by getting approval from others for all final decisions.

Consequently, tentativeness pervades the initial approach to negotiations. Even when the Chinese say that the time is at last ripe for serious negotiations, they convey the impression that those who do the talking will not be the ones who will do the deciding. Even before the actual sessions begin, the Chinese make the point that their negotiators are only agents of the ultimate decisionmakers. They also make it clear that no foreigner will be given information about the workings of that highly secret decisionmaking process.

Most of the businessmen interviewed commented on their feelings of uncertainty as they started their negotiations. Several described feeling as if they were plunging into the dark, or starting off without much of a chart. Most found some reassurance for their insecurity by talking to other foreign businessmen and discovering that they all were equally anxious and uncertain as they moved beyond introductions to their first negotiating moves with the Chinese.

III. THE OPENING MOVES

Once the American businessman has received permission to enter China, has found the right officials to do business with, and the proper atmosphere for negotiations has been established, the first substantive step is usually for the Chinese to request that the American explain what he has to offer, to put on the seminar or briefing.

YOU SHOW YOUR HAND FIRST

It is basic to the Chinese negotiating style to insist that the other party reveal its interests first while the Chinese mask their interests and priorities. Several respondents commented that from the beginning to the end of their negotiations they were never sure what the Chinese priorities were, and that the degree of interest displayed by those they were dealing with often was not a good indicator of ultimate Chinese decisions.

In one case, for example

> We brought out to Beijing a team of 20 for the negotiations I had set up. Our engineers put on a first-class performance, and some of their technical people showed great interest and asked a lot of questions. But after a day or so it seemed like a completely academic exercise with most of the Chinese officials showing little interest. Even when we talked price, they seemed uninterested. I and our commercial people had pretty well decided it was going to be a bust, with only our engineers having a bit of fun lecturing. But then, to my complete amazement, the Chinese suddenly said they were ready to buy.

In another case an American businessman complained:

> During the entire time we put on our presentation the Chinese never gave a hint as to their priorities, and since we have, as you can imagine, quite a few things that might be of use to them, we were never sure what we ought to emphasize. We finally decided for ourselves what Chinese priorities ought to be and then tried to sell them on our priorities.

The masking of intensity of interest is, of course, the classic pose in bazaar bargaining. To show too much interest can only drive up the price. There are also certain recent and essentially bureaucratic reasons for why the Chinese insist the other party show its hand first. The Chinese bureaucracy is not a "nerves of government" in the sense that there is not an effective communications system insuring that all the parts are in contact with each other. Consequently Chinese negotiators are often completely uninformed as to how their dealings fit into the general picture. Therefore, instead of being provided with clear requirements and specifications as to what the central planners want, negotiators must report upward what they have found is available and then learn whether their superiors find it of value. Even with the degree of "decentralization" that allowed enterprises and municipalities to negotiate separately, Chinese negotiators still had to know it was inappropriate to determine autonomously what China should buy without first finding out all that might be purchased.

Undoubtedly, such considerations play a part in Chinese actions, but it is also true that the Chinese are uncertain about their priorities, partly because they are still learning what is available from the advanced economies of the world. It is obvious that the Chinese are anxious to use seminars to learn as much as possible about various advanced technologies. Several respondents reported that they were presenting their seminar on one floor of the Peking Hotel, while competitor companies were doing the same thing at the same time on other floors, and the Chinese were going from one to the other, suggesting to each rival company that the others were revealing more technical secrets. American companies, with their traditions of competitiveness and their legal restraints against working together, are peculiarly vulnerable to being played off against each other. Although the Chinese have tried to do the same thing with Japanese companies, the Japanese will not play their game; instead they decide among themselves which one should have each contract, and the others simply withdraw and leave the Chinese with only one company to deal with. Not surprisingly, the Chinese see the Americans as more disorganized and easier to bargain with.

At times the Chinese demand that the seller display his wares first takes the form of an intelligence operation. Usually the objective is to learn a company's trade secrets, but in some cases the technologies they seek are protected by law for U.S. national security reasons. Two of the high technology firms, working in different fields, reported that the Chinese pressured them for such national security secrets, claiming that other American companies had revealed more than they had, even though they had gone to the very edge of the legal limits. In both cases the American representatives said that they believe that their competitors had probably broken the law; such is the Chinese ability to plant suspicion.

It is paradoxical that the Chinese should place a high value on "only the best" but have almost no appreciation for the monetary value of knowledge. The concept of proprietary rights seems to provoke suspicion among Chinese officials, because they believe the other party is holding back and not being forthright in the relationship. Among friends there should be no need for secrets. Furthermore, the Chinese believe that the bigger and more successful the company, the more willing it should be to share its knowledge at no cost to China. In fairness to the Chinese it should be noted that American behavior provides some grounds for these Chinese expectations. The bigger American corporations, as well as the larger American universities, have been exceedingly generous in providing free information to the Chinese.

Because of the potential for misunderstandings in Sino-American relations, it is worth emphasizing the Chinese tendency to undervalue the costs of knowledge. On the one hand they do not seem to appreciate whatever knowledge they are given, accepting it as their rightful due; on the other hand, they may become resentful when they are denied free access to knowledge they feel they deserve. American companies, and the U.S. government, have often heightened the potential for such Chinese misunderstandings by pretending to be more generous than they in fact can be. American enthusiasm to teach the Chinese often leads to boasting about the wonders of our knowledge and our way of life. The Chinese seem to be in great need of information and for Americans it is gratifying to be able to bring enlightenment to the uninitiated. Americans easily become carried away in elaborating on the state of the art in their field of knowledge.

Japanese companies seem to be more protective of their proprietary rights than Americans. This is odd, for not many years ago it was the Japanese who were widely charged with copying American technology. However, in the postwar years Japanese industries became very active in buying and licensing American technological innovations, and more recently they have made heavy R&D investments of their own. Consequently they are now conscious of the costs of effective ideas and techniques. As an official of one of the leading Japanese companies said, after admitting that at one time the Japanese also did not appreciate the financial aspects of patents and inventions:

> The Chinese do not understand the costs of R&D, and since they do not understand the value of knowledge there will be big trouble in time. They do not want to pay licensing fees, they do not honor patents, and they openly say they want to copy what we went to great pains to develop. We therefore have to be especially careful with them. We feel that some American companies may not realize what they are doing, and they are going to make trouble for themselves and for America's balance of payments.

Technology transferral to the PRC is a complex matter that implicitly touches on a great deal of trade negotiations with China. How far should Americans go in explaining their process to the Chinese, particularly given the Chinese demand that they should be taught not just how to use what is being sold but also how it is made? To what degree should the U.S. government encourage technological transfers to China at discount rates? These are questions that deserve careful answers. They are the kinds of questions that arise as a result of the Chinese practice of requiring American companies to explain their technology as a first step in the negotiating process.

Closely related to the Chinese desire for free information is their openness in admitting that whenever possible they will ignore patents and, after paying for only a single model, will try to copy it. The Chinese commitment to taking apart a model and replicating all of its parts may not be economical in terms of the total costs of time, energy, and scarce talent employed, but it does save foreign exchange—and it is very irritating to American sellers of such technologies. Although the Gang of Four have been "smashed" and Maoist doctrines of self-reliance are no longer Chinese orthodoxies, the Chinese have a deep cultural belief that copying and adapting foreign ways are quite legitimate and no acknowledgments need be made. For how else can Chinese expect to modernize than by skillfully selecting among Western techniques?

The closest the Chinese come to paying for knowledge is to ask for joint ventures and to suggest that through such cooperation the foreign firm can help teach the Chinese; in return the Chinese will provide cheap labor. Up until now this has not been an attractive bargain.

Another difficulty is that American negotiating teams are often under great strain to satisfy both technological and commercial questions simultaneously. Since late 1979, the Chinese, partly to accumulate information but also to insure the purchase of relevant technologies, have allowed an increasing degree of decentralization so that representatives of the end-users, the actual engineers from specific plants, are frequently present at the negotiations. At the same time the Chinese team will be composed of representatives from the universities or one of the commissions dealing with technical matters.

In spite of this tilting toward the technical, the American negotiators are well aware that ultimately any decision by the Chinese to buy will require clearance from the Bank of China if any substantive allocation of foreign exchange is involved. This situation calls for a presentation on all aspects of the potential transaction, but in the setting of the seminars it is most congenial to focus on explaining the state of the art. Most businessmen recognize that just satisfying Chinese curiosities will not guarantee a sale. Therefore, American negotiating teams try to introduce the commercial and financial considerations into their presentations, but this can be extremely difficult because so little is known about Chinese priorities and accounting principles. It is hard to tell whether Chinese are most responsive to capital outlay figures, cost-effectiveness considerations, servicing expenses, or the particular mix of tradeoffs that relates to efficiency and profitability.

Given the Chinese interest in technological processes and uncertainty about Chinese ways of economic thinking, the presentation seminars can become somewhat diffuse and at times lacking in focus. A representative of a major American enterprise confessed that one such session became

> the damnedest jumble of engineering jargon and economics double-talk you ever heard because we were trying to make sure that nothing was left uncovered, and that whatever the Chinese might want to hear they would hear it.

In many cases the first step in formal negotiations is not a technical seminar but a description by the American company of its entire line of products and services and suggestions on how they might be of value for China's modernization goals. Often these presentations involve a great deal of careful preparation and even costly research. One company, for example, worked out a complete plan for establishing a Chinese network of light aircraft communications that would link the main centers and facilitate the movement of officials throughout the country. An American company that manufactures trucks has provided the Chinese with an orderly plan for building up the nation's highway trucking capabilities.

In these two examples, as in most such situations, the Chinese had previously indicated little interest in national systems for light aircraft or trucking, but the Americans believed that they had plans that the Chinese ought to be interested in. Consequently, in trying to sell such proposals it is easy for American businessmen to overstate the benefits they believe they can bring to the Chinese.

The dynamics of this situation are such that the Chinese, quite understandably, must begin by putting up sales resistance because the total number of American proposals far exceeds Chinese capabilities to pay. In some respects the United States has contributed to this imbalance between enthusiastic Americans overselling their ability to help China and the Chinese need to be wary. For example, Washington's approval in the fall of 1980 of about 400 licenses for American companies to sell dual-use technology clearly provides the Chinese with a wider range of choices than they can possibly buy, especially after Beijing cut its 1981 military budget by $2 billion because of overspending in the 1979 war with Vietnam.[1]

The major Japanese trading companies do not have this problem because the range of what they have to sell and would like to buy need not be packaged in such discrete plans. Instead, the Japanese begin by examining known Chinese plans in careful detail and then seek to fit their offerings into those plans. Precisely because they are more diversified, it is efficient for them to engage in fundamental research about Chinese planning. American companies, with their far narrower range of specialization, can only hope that they can catch the Chinese interest.

FIRST GENERAL PRINCIPLES AND ONLY THEN THE DETAILS

Once the foreigner has shown his hand and the stage has been set for substantive negotiations, the Chinese seek agreement on generalities, dwelling on overall considerations, and avoiding specific details as much as possible, leaving, as they like to say, "concrete arrangements" to later negotiations. In trading relations their emphasis upon general principles first can take the extreme form of suggesting that the parties should agree to work toward a joint venture. The more usual general agreement proposal is a vaguely worded document indicating the intentions or the long-run interest of both parties in developing a contractual relationship. This insistence on first achieving agreement on general principles is one of the most distinctive characteristics of the Chinese negotiating style, and it has been noted by a State Department foreign service officer with considerable experience in observing Chinese negotiating practices and great knowledge of Chinese language and culture.[2] The Chinese approach is almost the exact opposite of the American belief that progress in negotiations is usually best facilitated by adhering to concrete and specific details, avoiding debates about generalities, which can easily become entangled in political or philosophical differences.

While the United States and China were negotiating as adversaries, this difference in style did cause considerable difficulties. During the Korean truce talks and the years of the Ambassadorial Talks, the Chinese generally tried to push for agreement along general principles that the United States could not accept because usually such agreements would have been seen as steps toward recognition of the

---

[1]*New York Times,* September 11, 1980.

[2]Charles W. Freeman, Jr., "Notes on Chinese Negotiating Styles," mimeograph, East Asian Legal Studies, Harvard Law School, June 1975.

PRC and the abandonment of Taiwan. On numerous occasions the United States tried to improve relations with the PRC by seeking agreement on very limited concrete matters such as allowing newsmen to enter the other's country. The Chinese rejected such concrete proposals by either calling for prior agreement on such larger matters as the status of Taiwan or raising other complicating issues that were usually associated with their ultimate goals.

In retrospect, when President Eisenhower successfully revived the Ambassadorial Talks it is significant that he instructed Ambassador Jacob Beam to avoid any discussion of specific issues and to try to have a "man-to-man" talk, for he was sure that Beam and the Chinese Ambassador would be able to find a basis for enduring relations at the personal level. Consequently the talks were revived, but they ran into trouble when President Kennedy sought to improve relations by emphasizing the American concern about limited and concrete issues.[3]

Once the adversary relationship was over, American diplomats and businessmen found the Chinese approach quite congenial. This will continue to be the case if the Chinese want agreements and do not invent stumbling blocks.

In diplomatic relations the Chinese practice of beginning with a search for agreement on generalities has been enthusiastically welcomed by American officials who have been ecstatic about the ease with which they have hit it off with high Chinese officials. Indeed, Kissinger admits that his first "negotiations" with Mao Zedong and Zhou Enlai were among the most exhilarating experiences he ever had in foreign affairs. The Kissinger meetings conformed to the standard pattern of Chinese sessions with high foreign officials: The Chinese begin with a tour of the world political scene, stressing points of policy agreement but exploring no subject in such depth as to expose latent differences. When such differences are too obvious to be completely ignored they noddingly acknowledge, "This is a matter on which we have different views." The end result is a shared spirit of agreement that sets the stage for more explicit general principle agreements such as, with Kissinger and Nixon, the Shanghai Communique.

In business negotiations the search for agreement on general principles usually starts with the Chinese admitting that because of the Gang of Four and other reasons, the particular area of concern is not advanced as it should be, the Chinese now want some foreign involve-

---

[3]Kenneth Young's study is a fascinating account of how the two countries, either intentionally or unintentionally, tragically caused each other constant trouble because of differences in this aspect of negotiating style. For a detailed but more limited analysis of Chinese adversary negotiating practices, see Robert B. Ekvall, *The Faithful Echo*, Twayne Publishers, New York, 1960.

ment, and they are therefore prepared to reach a general understanding in the hope that more concrete agreements will follow.

The Chinese value the negotiating tactic of first seeking agreement on general principles for several reasons. First, the wording of the general principles often makes it possible to extract concessions. If the other party complains that some principle is unacceptable because of how it might be interpreted in a particular situation, the Chinese generally respond by saying such matters of detail involve the concrete arrangements that are to be worked out later, and what is important at the beginning is for both sides to show mutual respect by agreeing to the principles. Several businessmen reported that they preferred to go along with what they hoped were innocuous sentiments rather than to create trouble at the very start of negotiations. As one of them said, "You do not want to cause waves right off the bat so you are inclined to side with the Chinese purpose—but it is damned surprising how much they can end up proposing in those first negotiating sessions."

The second advantage for the Chinese is that they can at times quickly turn an agreement on principles into an agreement on goals and then insist that all discussion on concrete arrangements must foster those agreed-upon goals. Although in most spheres of their culture the Chinese are not sticklers for logic, they are skilled in their negotiating practices in exploiting any and all logical contradictions by the other party. As one businessmen with many hours of negotiating experience explained,

> By making each agreement between us move from a more general to a more technical level, the Chinese could constantly argue that what they were insisting upon in operating procedures was logically consistent with all that had been agreed to before. I don't think they won out very much by doing it this way, but they sure taxed our patience and always put us on the defensive.

Most important of all, the Chinese demand for agreement on principles first can be used later to attack the other party for bad faith and for violating the spirit of the principles. This can involve more than just questions of logical consistency or legalistic correctness, for the Chinese can thereby claim moral superiority and suggest that the other party is behaving dishonorably, as a renegade, a cheat, or a fair weather friend.

During the years between President Nixon's first visit and the final consummation of "normalization" on January 1, 1979, the Chinese repeatedly charged that concrete proposals or actions by Washington "violated the spirit of the Shanghai Communique." Since normalization, the Chinese have held up the "spirit" of the Normalization Communique as the proper criterion for criticizing what they find displeasing in specific American actions. The same thing has occurred in Chinese negotiating tactics with other countries. For example, during the negotiations on a Sino-Japanese shipping agreement, the Chinese raised an issue that the Japanese had to reject immediately.

> The Chinese negotiating team looked offended and stated that such an argument was contrary to the spirit of the Joint Communique signed in 1972, that China had to seriously question the "political philosophy" of the Japanese negotiator.[4]

Businessmen also report that the Chinese sometimes put pressure on them when discussing the final concrete arrangements by suggesting that they have broken the spirit of friendship in which the business relationship was originally established. The ploy, of course, allows the Chinese to play the role of the innocent and aggrieved party while adopting an aggressive and prickly manner, designed to intimidate the other party. Presumably the objective is to shame the other party into becoming more yielding on the substantive details of the negotiations.

This ploy need not be particularly effective if the other party is prepared to stand firm and ignore Chinese criticisms. It can usually be assumed that if the Chinese cannot get their way by citing the spirit of an initial agreement, they will in time focus on the problems at hand. Several businessmen did suggest that they were somewhat unnerved by the Chinese challenge that they were not acting in the right spirit and they even suspected that possibly the Chinese were preparing to break off negotiations and turn to a company more willing to be friendly. Also, of course, many of the negotiators were under dual pressures because the presidents of their companies had agreed to the general principles, and they were therefore in the position of possibly embarrassing their home offices or of being ordered to make what they believed to be inappropriate concessions.

Although businessmen appear to have found no uniform technique for coping with the problems of moving from agreed-upon general principles to concrete details, those who spoke to this issue unanimously insisted that their relations with the Chinese were never really damaged by firm adherence to their position on specific questions. Furthermore, several businessmen cited examples of how very easy it was to smooth ruffled Chinese feathers over "violations" of the

---

[4]Ogura Kazuo, "How the 'Inscrutables' Negotiate with the 'Inscrutables': Chinese Negotiating Tactics *Vis-à-Vis* the Japanese," *China Quarterly*, No. 79, September 1979, p. 530.

spirit of agreements by symbolic gestures of continuing good will, even as they held firm on matters of detail.

The executive of a large American corporation told of how he was having trouble negotiating the costs of the training program associated with a large contract, and of how the Chinese began to accuse him of not staying in line with the spirit of their basic agreement. He explained, "I was finally able to restore peace with the Chinese when I was able to show them some public relations materials on our work with the Chinese that had just been finished by our graphic arts people back home."

One of the major Japanese trading firms was denounced for abridging the spirit of their contract when they had difficulties in negotiating the cost of labor. The Chinese insisted that their workers should be costed at "world standards" even though they would be paid at Chinese wage rates and the Chinese government would get the difference; but the Chinese would agree to pay only $100 a day to the Japanese engineers on the project because "China is a poor country and cannot meet world standards." The problem was resolved when the Japanese accepted the Chinese costs for labor and then conspicuously added elsewhere in the contract the precise cost of the Japanese engineers. The Japanese then published several articles praising the entire enterprise and the Chinese role in carrying it out, which smoothed the matter over.[5]

It is not difficult to explain the apparent contradiction between the Chinese insistence that agreement on general principles should precede discussion of concrete arrangements and the ease with which foreign negotiators have been able to overcome Chinese objections that the principles are not being followed. The Chinese attach great importance to symbols and symbolic matters. Symbols, such as the spirit of an agreement, have a reality for the Chinese. This tendency also works in reverse. Symbolic responses are also seen as being substantively significant. As long as the other party acknowledges commitment to the spirit of the agreement, the Chinese feel inhibited in complaining over differences in the interpretation of details.

In government-to-government relations the Chinese make an even greater point of agreeing first on general principles than they do in

---

[5]The Chinese are currently following the practice of setting higher wages for labor under joint venture contracts but actually paying the worker according to domestic wage scales. For example, in the joint venture signed with Schindler Halding (a Swiss elevator company) and Jardine's of Hong Kong to produce elevators in China, the wages for laborers will be US $1,360 per person per year for the first five years and then US $2,176 thereafter. In this case the difference between the contract figure and the amount to be received by the workers is said to cover the cost of welfare, medical, and other benefits customarily provided by the state. See "China Swiss-Hong Kong Joint Venture Contract Made Public," *China Newsletter,* No. 26, June 1980, Jetro (Japan External Trade Organization), pp. 23-25.

commercial negotiations. And, of course, they have repeatedly criticized the actions of others as being in violation of the spirit of what they see as the fundamental agreement. What is not as clear is whether they can be as easily satisfied in the political-diplomatic realm as they are in commercial dealing with appropriate symbolic responses. After first the Shanghai Communique and then the agreement on normalization, Washington has gone to great lengths to make concrete actions conform to the spirit of these agreements but has chosen to do little about symbolic manipulations. In the case of Japan, the very process of arriving at an initial agreement involved a prolonged struggle over the anti-hegemony clause, and subsequent Sino-Japanese relations have had a clearly defined symbolic as well as concrete level of interaction. By skillfully handling the symbolic dimension of the relationship, the Japanese have not had to be quite as careful as the U.S. government has been in bargaining on such substantive matters as Taiwan relations, reciprocity in cultural exchanges, and the like.

AMBIGUITY ABOUT LETTERS OF INTENT

The Chinese practice of seeking agreement on general principles often takes the form of signing what have been called letters of intent, letters of interest, or protocols. Because of a foreign exchange crisis in 1979 a significant change in the use of such letters may in time affect Chinese negotiating practices.

The standard procedure after the Cultural Revolution was for nearly all contractual negotiations to begin with a letter of intent (or interest or a protocol), which was a formalization of the Chinese desire for an agreement on principles. Such letters usually indicated the intended relationship and included vague references to the sums of money to be involved and relevant dates. In many cases foreign firms anxious to engage in trade used such agreement for commercial value to improve the value of their stocks or otherwise to raise money in the capital market. In 1979 when Beijing realized that through the uncontrolled signing of letters of intent China had committed itself to spending nearly $60 billion, the regime had no alternative but to cancel or postpone all agreements and to review which ones would be honored.

By mid-1980 there was considerable confusion about the significance of such letters. Most businessmen interviewed have taken the view, largely in reaction to the Chinese cancellations and postponements of the earlier letters, that such commitments should not be taken at face value, and that in negotiations with the Chinese nothing should be considered final until it has actually been realized. According to these businessmen, it may be necessary to humor the Chinese by going along with the stage of signing papers that may have no binding powers but that can open the door to more substantive negotiations. As one such businessman explained, "I had to repeatedly telex New York so that they should not waste time or money by asking the legal department to go over the document line by line. I also had to warn them not to get production excited."

A minority of the businessmen were convinced that the Chinese are still going through a learning process, which will result in more legalistic procedures. Hence the agreements on general principles contained in such letters of intent must be taken seriously.

Whether majority or minority opinion will prove correct will depend in large measure on how successful the Chinese become in neutralizing foreign trade decisionmaking. All parties generally agree that negotiations starting at the enterprise level tend to produce more realistic initial agreements than those involving high-level administrative cadres.

The future importance of letters of intent is also affected by the ambivalent Chinese attitudes toward publicity about agreements with foreign enterprises. Announcement of negotiating successes may influence investors, attract potential subcontractors, raise morale within the company, reassure top management, facilitate bank financing, and generally provide good public relations. Publicity is especially important in getting contracts for hotel construction, which necessitate appeals to capital markets for funding, and for banks, which compete in attracting customers for the China trade. The value of publicity for some American companies is further heightened if management has decided to forgo the prospects of actual profits in China trade in return for the immediate benefits of greater prestige and world-wide visibility.

In government-to-government relations there is a similar American bias in favor of publicity. Cabinet members and heads of agencies and offices want publicity for their visits to China; and there is competition among officials to reach agreements with the Chinese. Dr. Frank Press, President Carter's Science Advisor, welcomed publicity for the 1978 agreement on cultural and scientific exchange with the PRC, even though it contained unrealistic figures for exchange and he had no powers to oblige American universities to accept Chinese students.

The Chinese have mixed feelings concerning publicity about impending commercial agreements. To a limited extent they are anxious to publicize progress in foreign trade negotiations because such news suggests that modernization is achievable and that China has become a significant actor in the world economy. Publicity about impending agreements with one company can also stimulate other companies to take a greater interest in China trading, hence generally strengthen China's bargaining position. The Chinese have been eager to generate publicity about joint ventures with Overseas Chinese in no small part because Western and Japanese firms have been skeptical about such arrangements. It is the Chinese, in contrast to the foreign traders, who enthusiastically boast about the number of impending contracts to come out of each year's semiannual trade fairs.

The Chinese are nevertheless strongly inclined to secrecy throughout the negotiating process. Chinese bureaucrats, like bureaucrats in most countries, have an instinctive distrust of all types of publicity. More particularly, they recognize that publicity can become a form of pressure on them during subsequent negotiations. The foreign negotiator can argue that it would not look good for China to fail at something the world has expected to occur. Members of Chinese negotiating teams also can get into trouble with their superiors or with cadres in parallel ministries if they are seen as promoting themselves by publicizing their dealings with foreigners.

Secrecy also makes it easier for the Chinese to play off one company against another. Actually this objective is best served by a mix of publicity and secrecy so as to cause others to worry that perhaps they are missing out on significant developments without knowing precisely what they may be.

As several of the businessmen observed, the Chinese at the very beginning of negotiations attempt to control the limits of both publicity and secrecy, yet they do not seem to have firm guidelines on precisely where they want the boundaries to be set. The very fact that they are interested in using a mix for ad hoc advantages produces uncertainty among foreign traders as to what can or should be announced about the first stages of negotiations. The Chinese may treat violations of confidentiality as major breaches of faith, but they may also take failure to publicize intended deals as a slight.

Chinese attitudes about publicity and secrecy can leave American negotiators in a quandary as they reach agreement on general principles. The problem is made more difficult by the usual refusal of the Chinese to provide precise answers as to their preferences. A man who negotiated a major contract for building some plants in China described his experience in the following way:

> After we had reached agreement on the general plan, I asked the chief negotiator from the Third Machine Tool Ministry whether we should issue a joint statement. He said it would not be necessary but that if we wished to announce what our company hoped to do, that

was, of course, our business. He added, however, that we should not say anything on any of the delicate matters. Since we had not yet got down to real details, I didn't know what might be considered delicate. I did draw up a press release and asked the Chinese to approve it. Their response was typical in that they said it was good to have the press release, but then they showed themselves to be uneasy about anything concrete. By asking us not to specify anything about the projected costs, the location, or the tentative dates for starting and finishing construction, the press release could only create a sense of mystery. We were uncomfortable because it might be seen that we were trying to claim more than we deserved.

Other American businessmen generally agree that this problem is a "no-win" situation. A few believe that the way the Chinese shift their views on publicity and secrecy is calculated to improve their bargaining position for the next round of discussions. The majority take a more understanding (or maybe more patronizing) view and suggest that the Chinese are genuinely unsure of what mix of publicity and secrecy they would prefer at the completion of the first phase of negotiations.

Japanese businessmen do not seem to have this problem because their own strategy calls for secrecy at all stages of negotiations. The large Japanese trading companies do not seek publicity on specific negotiations but rather publicize their aggregate trade with China. Collectively the Japanese are able to maintain the positive impression of expanding China trade, which the Chinese desire, through the publicity of their various trade associations. The only complaint of Japanese traders is that the Chinese have occasionally tried to exploit the tight-lipped Japanese policy by spreading adverse rumors during the negotiating process that the Japanese feel they cannot answer without creating greater problems.

The Chinese are inclined to be critical of their biggest trading partners and to extol the less important ones. Before Japan became China's largest trading partner, the Chinese praised Japanese technology and products more and criticized less; and today the Chinese have more praise for American products, but their enthusiasm seems to be declining as trade with America grows. The Chinese may believe that instead of generously praising those they do the most business with, their bargaining position can better be served by keeping such partners slightly uncomfortable so that they will not take their successes for granted. By publicly playing up to their lesser trading partners, the Chinese seem to be trying to encourage them to become more active in the future.

The Chinese have complex feelings about the dependency associated with a major trading partnership, and although they welcome the benefits, they are also quick to suspect that they are not getting their just returns. To sustain the interest and concern of the one on whom they are dependent they may feel the need to be provocative. China trade is less than 2 percent of Japan's foreign commerce but trade with Japan makes up 40 percent of China's foreign trade. That suggests it is the Chinese who have the most to lose, but the Chinese tend to be less complimentary of the Japanese.

THE LONG WAIT

In the opening phases of negotiations with the Chinese, the next problem foreign traders usually have is an unconscionably long wait between the initial agreement to go ahead and actual negotiations on specific details. According to all informants, here is where one must remember that the first rule in negotiating with the Chinese is the need for abiding patience. As Tsuneo Kawasakiya, General Manager of the China Department of Mitsui & Co., has said, "Our negotiators need physical stamina as well as tough mental powers."[6] Once an initial agreement has been reached, American negotiators become more than ever impatient for the consummation of a deal, for they tend to assume that the step from general agreement to detailed substantive negotiations should be a short one. In many cases, the impatience of the Americans is fueled by the fact that it is not convenient, or economical, to keep their entire negotiating team in China doing nothing.

For the Chinese, however, this may be the time for substantial delay. The officials who have been talking with the Americans may not have the authority to go further and must await instructions. The Chinese are also short of expert talent and thus lower officials may have to await the clearing of bottlenecks in their own hierarchies. Also, Chinese cadres often seem genuinely to feel that once there has been an agreement in principle, congratulations are in order, and therefore they are in no hurry to get into the potentially troublesome haggling over details.

Chinese stalling at this stage may also be a negotiating tactic. Believing that they have whetted the appetite of the foreign businessman, they may now feel that they can probably improve on price and quantity terms by allowing his impatience to work for the Chinese benefit.

---

[6]"Organizing for China Trade: The View from Japan," Address at Seminar on Doing Business with the People's Republic of China, Business International Institute/Asia, Hilton Hotel, Hong Kong, April 10-11, 1979, p. 16.

The Chinese seem quite convinced that they will always gain an advantage if they can repeatedly reaffirm that it is the other party who needs the agreement and that final agreement is not a pressing matter for China. This is the case in enough commercial and diplomatic negotiations that the Chinese have not had to reexamine this assumption. At times, as we have noted, some Americans have been able to reverse the pressure by threatening to leave China by a set date, hence forcing them into negotiations. But more often than not the Chinese prevail and the Americans simply have to live with their frustrations and to worry about whether they will get the final agreement. One major American firm that builds large chemical plants has waited three years after making its formal presentations and signing letters of intent for the Chinese to say they are ready to engage in the final, substantive negotiations. Each year their inquiries are answered with the same response, "Yes, we certainly do want to negotiate a final contract—maybe it will be next year." Especially frustrating is that the length of the waiting period provides no clues as to what the Chinese will ultimately decide they want. In some cases, the longer the wait the larger the contract; in other cases, more prompt responses produced disappointingly small purchases.

IV. THE SUBSTANTIVE NEGOTIATING SESSION

The Chinese understandably seek to carry into the negotiating sessions whatever advantages they may have gained in the preliminaries. Yet frequently the first substantive sessions reveal certain Chinese weaknesses that may not always work to the advantage of the other party. At this stage the Chinese often display a fascination for tactics that may be at the expense of any recognizable strategy. Some would classify this absorption with manipulation as the second most distinctive Chinese negotiating characteristics after their stress on agreement over general principles. Once the Chinese have achieved their general principles, it is often hard to discern precisely what they are after because of their use of ploys, tactics, and gamesmanship, often of a subtle nature, but frequently crude and transparent.

Chinese captivation with the pleasures of outwitting others and of gaining unexpected benefits for the self, following so closely upon their graciousness in hospitality, reinforces the image of the clever, if not devious, Chinese in the minds of American negotiators. The Chinese do have a well-deserved reputation for being skilled and hard headed negotiators. At times, however, this reputation may become a liability because it causes others to expect trickery where none exists —a clever move when in fact there is only confusion or indecision. The Chinese sometimes act in a way that leads others to wonder whether it is clumsiness or craft. Indeed, according to some of our respondents, the Chinese make such obviously self-serving demands that one immediately expects they must have some scheme afoot because otherwise they could not be taken seriously.

Frequently, Chinese negotiating strategy is no more than just the sum of whichever tactics have been successful. Respondents described numerous cases in which the Chinese moved directly from lofty concerns about general principles to haggling about random minutiae. To the Americans this suggested that the Chinese did not have much in the way of strategic plans. One businessman expressed his puzzlement at being unable to discern any Chinese negotiating strategy in these words: "Once we got down to details their negotiating team was full of petty games and tricks, and they seemed to have no strategy for getting to wherever they wanted to go."

This view may not be entirely fair to the Chinese. First, in advancing an underdeveloped economy one may not need an elaborate nego-

51

tiating strategy and plans beyond the simple objective of trying to get the most for the least cost. Second, it is not normal in Chinese culture to use the level of abstraction appropriate for explicit strategic discourse. The Chinese tendency is to operate either at a very high level of generalities (and moral abstractions) or at the concrete level, thereby largely avoiding the middle level of generalization so important in science-oriented cultures. It is not that the Chinese make no distinctions among goals (general principles), strategy, and tactics, for their literature on politics recognizes these three levels; rather they tend in negotiating practice to avoid statements about either their own or the other party's strategic or "middle level" concerns. They seem quite content to jump from almost fatuous abstractions of "general principles" to very concrete points of detail. This negotiating style leaves the other party quite uncertain about Chinese priorities, their possible fallback positions, or the ways in which the current negotiations might fit into any larger Chinese plans. In short, negotiations, once the general principles have been established, can quickly become swamped in detail.

The Chinese propensity to focus on items rather than programs, on tactics over strategy, means that negotiations tend to proceed with a great many ground rules unstated and considerable uncertainty as to exactly how the Chinese are likely to read progress or lack of progress in the negotiating process. Much of what occurs in the negotiations has a tacit quality, with each side assuming that it understands what the other is up to, but neither can be sure. Consequently, American negotiators frequently misjudge how well the negotiations are progressing. Without warning everything can come to a stop as the Chinese announce their lack of interest in proceeding further; or just as unexpectedly they may declare that they are ready to sign a contract, even though no specified contract has been presented.

SIZING UP THE NEGOTIATING TEAM

Leaders of Chinese negotiating teams will frequently begin substantive sessions with the flattering remark, "We have only known you a short time but we are already old friends," to which most Americans feel it necessary to give an enthusiastic affirmative response. The next ritualized move calls for the American to give an emphatic denial to the Chinese feigned self-deprecating remark, "We have much to learn from you because our work in this field is very backward." Building upon the feelings of obligation created by Chinese hospitality, the leader will end by saying, "We are counting upon you to help us achieve international standards as fast as possible for this is the goal of our Four Modernizations."

At the substantive sessions the Chinese negotiating teams are almost always larger than American or even Japanese teams. By this time most of the American engineers and technical people who participated in the presentation seminars have left China, but the Chinese technical personnel and representatives of the end-users often remain with their teams. (This has been particularly true since late 1979.)

Several American businessmen felt that a key early signal of the intensity of Chinese interest in doing business with them was the caliber of the Chinese assigned to their sessions. Because the Chinese are short of qualified interpreters, the assigning of a superior person could be taken as a fairly reliable indication of Chinese earnest. One businessman observed,

> Back in the first days of the Canton Trade Fair it was purely the luck of the draw what kind of an interpreter you might be stuck with. Now we can tell right away how serious they are by the ability of the person working the sessions. We have gotten to know pretty well who does what kind of work, and this does reduce the surprises a bit.

Although the quality of the interpreter may be a reliable indicator of Chinese intentions the size of the negotiating team may not. Frequently they seem to use negotiating sessions for either training or intelligence purposes, with the result that many people may be in the room, the questioning may be intense, but the results may not be substantial. Aside from the leaders of the Chinese team, the interpreter, and technical persons representing the end-user, it is often hard to tell the functions of the other members of the team. Probably somebody is there to keep an eye on the others. Furthermore, it is almost always impossible to know to whom the various members of the team report, and it is often difficult to determine exactly where the team leader belongs in the hierarchy of his ministry or trading corporation.

This uncertainty is related to a problem that many of our respondents claim to be the most troublesome in negotiating with the Chinese—namely, the vagueness of the actual authority of the Chinese negotiators. Frequently the Chinese will begin negotiations as though they were empowered to make all decisions, but when snags arise they will suddenly claim that they must refer all issues to higher authorities, which can block further progress for unpredictable lengths of time.

In the 19th century one of the most troublesome problems the West

had in the opening of China was precisely the question of the pleni-
potentiary powers of Chinese negotiators. It was bad enough that
Chinese diplomats were caught in a constant bind of having to
simultaneously negotiate with both the foreign power and the imperial court; but worse, officials could be severely punished if they caused
imperial displeasure. In the 1850s, for example, the newly established
diplomatic corps was completely undone when the emperor ordered
the execution of Chinese diplomats because the treaty they had negotiated with Russia at, of all places, Yalta, displeased him: How could
one press for negotiating advantages with the Chinese if they refused
to recognize the principle of diplomatic immunity, not just for foreign
diplomats but also for their own?[1]

Today cadres are in somewhat the same situation. It is to their
advantage to exaggerate their importance when talking with foreigners—especially when they can expect a personal gift. However,
they also know that their careers can be jeopardized and they can be
harshly punished if the results of their negotiations are criticized.
Hence, quite understandably, they back away from responsibility.
Furthermore, today there is no unambiguous higher source of appeal
capable of making quick and decisive decisions. A negotiating team
usually reports to another committee of officials who have similar
need to evade responsibility. One of the businessmen vividly described
the problem:

> You have no idea what power to make decisions the people you are
> negotiating with have; but even worse, they don't either. And if they
> have to get a decision from above then the problem is that the Chi-
> nese have no czar, no one man who can say yes or no. Instead they
> have layers of committees and your negotiators can even get mixed
> up and go to the wrong committee. Or at least it seems as though
> they are getting the runaround. Which means that you just have to
> wait and practice patience. It is patience, patience, patience!

Some American businessmen are troubled by their perceptions of
the personal difficulties of Chinese negotiators. The Americans feel it
is unfair that the Chinese cadres might personally suffer because of
the terms of the agreement. One man who has had extensive dealings
in Peking tells of his experiences:

> The old-timers on the negotiating teams have usually gone through
> enough hell so that they have had the starch taken out of them. I
> once was dealing with an old-timer who told me he had been in jail

---

[1]For the details of the Ili Controversy between China and Russia and the reactions
of the Peking diplomatic corps to Ambassador Chunghow's punishment of death by
decapitation, see Morse, Vol. II, Chapter XVI.

eight times. He certainly didn't want to cause any waves. The young-sters who have had everything given to them don't really give a damn. They just go through the eight-to-five motions, never any heavy lifting, and they stop instantly at quitting time. It can be very frustrating. You would like to make a scene, but you also feel sorry for them. In any case who are you to complain to? If you knew, you'd be dealing with them in the first place.

A somewhat different but not unrelated problem is the lack of experience and knowledge about customary practices in other coun-tries. Inexperience fosters tentativeness and the need to consult su-periors. The result again can be stalling and protracted indecision, which causes increased frustration, especially if the home office is constantly inquiring about how the negotiations are progressing.

Some American businessmen are worried about how long it may take for the Chinese to get around this problem of inexperience. They note in particular that the few qualified people are spread very thin, they have to be called into too many decisions, and the decisions tend to pile up. In the meantime Beijing seems determined to encourage increased commercial negotiations at a faster rate than people can be trained. Officials are being exposed to threatening situations before they can build up their confidence, with the result that China is ac-cumulating bureaucrats who believe that prudence demands hyper-cautiousness. The learning process for Chinese officials is not increasing the numbers of competent decisionmakers, only swelling the ranks of bureaucrats.

These problems all point to a paradoxical contrast in the character of typical Chinese and American negotiating teams. In the prelimi-nary stages, it is the Chinese who stress personal interaction and friendship; when serious negotiating begins the Chinese side usually becomes highly bureaucratized, requiring coordination with layers of hierarchical committees and senior officials. Americans at the early stages may use elaborate teams in making technical presentations, but when serious negotiating begins the American instinct is to move toward a one-on-one relationship; hence American negotiators tend to be lone individuals or at most a team of only two or three men with a definitive spokesman.

Americans instinctively clarify lines of responsibility, Chinese blur them. Therefore, American negotiators generally know precisely the limits of their mandates, and they are anxious to communicate these limits clearly to the Chinese. The Chinese, as already mentioned, usu-ally give vague and conflicting signals as to the limits of their nego-tiating authority.

The Japanese traders seem to have no difficulties with respect to the size, the ambiguous authority, and the tentativeness of the

Chinese negotiators. Representatives of what were once called the "friendly firms" would never criticize the Chinese on any score. The large Japanese trading companies also have none of the complaints voiced by the Americans. The several reasons why this is the case all point to certain advantages the Japanese have in trading with China.

The Japanese uniformly maintain far larger staffs in China than American companies do, and consequently they have greater flexibility in adjusting to Chinese scheduling whims and irregularities in the tempo of negotiations. If negotiations should stall in one area, manpower can be shifted to other projects, and, consequently, the Japanese firms are less frustrated by Chinese indecision. The costs of posting people to Beijing are considerably less for Japanese companies than for American companies, and it is far easier for the Japanese to rotate people in and out of China. In the summer of 1980, for example, Mitsui had five men assigned to its Beijing office, but it also had an additional 40 or so men who were rotated in for three months to one year on tourist visas. In Tokyo, Mitsui has nearly 400 people working on China trade. Like the other large Japanese trading companies, Mitsui has a wide range of import and export interests and therefore they can readily orchestrate their negotiations and transfer skilled manpower to or from different contractual possibilities according to changing Chinese interests. American firms are, of course, limited to particular lines of enterprise, and they are thus more vulnerable to shifting Chinese interests and priorities.

Furthermore, although none of the Japanese trading company officials would admit to such practices, the large Japanese conglomerates have the capacity to confront Chinese foot-dragging in one set of negotiations by threatening to delay negotiations in other areas where the Chinese have a greater sense of urgency. Rather than acknowledging the use of such threats, the Japanese prefer to stress the positive, as they see it, and claim credit for being able to satisfy a wider range of Chinese needs more quickly and easily than individual American companies can. Mitsui, for example, takes considerable pride in its ability, through its satellite communications system tied in with computers at 164 offices throughout the world, to respond almost instantly to Chinese requests for purchases of almost anything. If, say, the Chinese National Metals and Minerals Import-Export Corporation wanted to purchase a cargo of scrap steel, the Mitsui office in Beijing could give the Chinese in a few minutes, and certainly by the start of business the next day, exact price quotations and delivery dates of whatever scrap steel is available for sale in the world.

The "big four" Japanese trading companies—Mitsui, Mitsubishi, Marubeni, and Itoh—with more than 200 employees in China are in quite a different situation from that of even the largest American companies and financial institutions with their negotiating teams of two or three people. The Japanese companies are engaged in multiple negotiations, and they also are far more effectively coordinated than the Chinese, given their problems of communications among bureaucracies.

Understandably, the Japanese firms manifest greater self-confidence and less anxiety about offending Chinese negotiators than the typical American negotiator. Hence the Japanese tend to be much more aggressive—some Americans would say more arrogant—in sizing up the Chinese negotiating teams and concluding that they should teach the Chinese the "international standards" of commerce. They argue that China's modernization requires the Chinese become a part of the international trading community and the faster the better; therefore, even though it may be painful for the Chinese to have to change their practices, they will benefit if they learn from the Japanese. Right from the first substantive negotiating sessions the Japanese seek to take command, whereas the Americans feel compelled to sell themselves and are prone to make claims beyond their ability to deliver.

The Japanese also see the benefits of encouraging the Chinese to develop dependency feelings toward them. It is not just that the Japanese are more authoritative and hence have some legitimate claim to the role of teacher, but also the balance of trade is such that Japan represents 40 percent of China's foreign trade, while China constitutes only 2.5 percent of Japan's foreign trade. Most Japanese negotiators know these statistics, and they do not behave the same as some American negotiators, who may worry about being blamed if anything should go wrong after the heads of their companies had successfully opened trade with China.

PRICES, PROFITS, AND MYTHS
ABOUT CAPITALISM

Once the discussions are engaged, Chinese negotiators seem to want no uncertainty about the price of what they are buying or selling. Repeatedly the businessmen commented, "the Chinese are realists, they know the bottom line is price." Yet, they are sensitive to quality, wanting only the best. Considerations of pride and fear of subsequent criticisms for accepting poor quality products thus clash with the imperative of price, all of which compels Chinese negotiators to demand and expect to get exceptional bargains.

Concentration on unit price is so great among Chinese negotiators that they have little mind for other considerations. Several of the American businessmen believed that this propensity will cause China severe problems in the future. They argue that the Chinese, guided so much by price calculations, are procuring a wide assortment of plants and machinery with no concern about the long-run problems of standardization. With their bargain purchases, the Chinese have been accumulating a stock of incompatible industrial equipment that will manufacture possibly incompatible products. This problem is further exaggerated by the Chinese practice of reverse engineering—copying foreign products without permission or licensing. All these propensities reflect a short-run concept of price and little understanding of costs.

Several of the American businessmen, and uniformly the Japanese traders, reported that the Chinese have become sophisticated more rapidly about quality than about financing. Seemingly there are more qualified Chinese doing their homework on technical and engineering questions than there are economists and accountants. Reportedly fewer members of Chinese negotiating teams appreciate the significance of all the variables that go into the financing of purchases and should affect judgment about prices. The Chinese tend to concentrate on only two variables, the unit price and the base interest rate, if credits are called for. They are less impressed with other considerations customarily related to price such as the tradeoffs among speed of delivery, extent of servicing arrangements, volume discounts, and the like.

The Chinese tendency to treat price without regard to time considerations is a direct result of their operating for so long in a socialist economy, where their officials discount the cost of capital. Until recently plant managers received capital from the state as outright grants; they were not required to amortize capital investments. Therefore it is not surprising that Chinese officials are generally insensitive to the costs of tying up capital for long periods without obtaining a return on investment. Chinese negotiators generally seem to have no guidelines for deciding how important it is that the machinery of a plant will be in full production in six months, a year, 18 months, or two years. Low price is paramount.

Chinese insensitivity to the relationship between time and costs contributes to, but also works against, one of the most common Chinese negotiating ploys, that of stalling. For reasons already noted, ranging from American impatience to the bureaucratic need of the Chinese to diffuse responsibility, whenever in doubt and whenever they wish to increase pressure on the other party, the Chinese are prone to slow down or even postpone negotiations. It seems rarely to cross the Chinese mind that such tactics might be costly to them, particularly at a time of unrelenting inflation. Rarely do the Chinese show appreciation for the possibility that they ought to move faster before another round of price rises occurs.

Several American businessmen told of cases in which the Chinese broke off negotiations, complaining about prices, and then a year or so later reopened talks only to be dumbfounded and then suspicious when told that now the price was even higher.

The supremacy of price considerations also contributes to erratic behavior and the otherwise unexplainable cancellations of negotiations and even of signed contracts. Leaving aside the retrenchment move of 1979 in which large numbers of contracts were canceled or shelved, there have been many cases in which foreign firms have had contracts canceled with the only explanation being vague references to price considerations. In most of these cases the foreign negotiators succeeded in convincing the Chinese that it was in China's interest to go ahead with the deal even if it meant indebtedness, but apparently the Chinese negotiators were unable subsequently to make a convincing case with their higher officials who had less sophisticated understanding of costs. On other occasions the Chinese have been temporarily carried away with the idea of working with the world's "best," for example in building hotels or establishing a trade center, but then considerations of price arose as the Chinese asked themselves why pay the costs of a world class hotel or trade center when it is possible to charge world class prices for the locally produced version.[2]

When the Chinese are selling they are, of course, not at all unaware of the trend in world prices. In these situations they note consumer market prices of the item in foreign countries and propose that the Chinese sale price should be near to that figure, allowing the trader only what the Chinese consider to be a "fair" profit. Here again there is a problem of inexperience, in that the Chinese have little under-

---

[2]The story of the cancellation of the $250 million foreign trade center in Beijing is revealing both about the Chinese concern for price and the problems of Chinese negotiators with other elements in their bureaucracy. The Ministry of Foreign Trade, after more than two years of negotiations with Japanese firms, agreed to a contract with an American group composed of Turner International of New York, Gerald Hines of Houston, Kaiser Engineering, to be financed by Chase Manhattan Bank. The Americans apparently won out by convincing the Foreign Trade Ministry negotiators that it would be possible to erect a more expensive complex than the Japanese had proposed. Because of the cost the project came under criticism at the September 1980 sessions of the National People's Congress. Furthermore the Beijing city government strongly opposed the plan, largely because it included no direct financial benefits for the city itself. This combined opposition was strong enough so that, even after construction had begun and the Chinese had committed $7 million, the Foreign Trade Ministry terminated the project. For some of the details, see Fox Butterfield, *New York Times*, October 1, 1980, p. D1.

standing of the complex processes of distribution and marketing in the outside world.

The Chinese are deeply suspicious about profits in a capitalist system. The combination of their Marxist dogma and their traditional peasant's distrust of merchants convinces them that profits are nothing more than the returns from cheating customers. They accept the fact that capitalist businessmen believe they need a profit, but they also feel that such businessmen should be "well mannered" and not "greedy." In spite of all the changes in China since Mao, the idea of dealing with "evil" capitalists seems still to arouse a peculiar blend of anxiety, self-righteousness, and suspicion among Chinese officials. On the one hand they tend to picture capitalists as shrewd tricksters who would never agree to a price if it did not bring a handsome profit. On the other hand they think of themselves as the deserving poor of whom the rich should not take advantage. Hence there is always a need to nudge the conscience of the capitalists. Precisely because America and Japan are rich their companies should give China better terms, or so the Chinese seem to believe.

Thus in a strange way the backwardness of China reinforces the old Middle Kingdom complex and leads Chinese negotiators to expect others to acknowledge that China is exceptionally deserving and should be given discount prices and special consideration. The Chinese have even insisted that the other party is "unfriendly" if it does not give special treatment to China.

The Chinese feel that they deserve special treatment but they also fear that foreigners will take advantage of them. Their instinct is to plead "Please don't skin us alive" and to try to surmount their fears by seeking out "friends" who will not cheat them or prestigious firms who they hope will not stoop to unfair practices.

These considerations suggest that the sensitivity of the Chinese to price reflects more than just the Communist principles of political economy. It probably taps a deep psychological fear of being cheated by dangerous foreigners and competes with the equally strong desire to be protected by the understanding foreigners. This anxiety may explain the peculiar negotiating atmosphere that many businessmen described in which the Chinese seem to be simultaneously extremely suspicious and also anxious for friendship and understanding. The Chinese seem to yearn to transform the inherently adversary character of negotiations into a sheltering relationship. American and Japanese accounts indicate the Chinese negotiators generally hope that the foreigners will provide them with a shield to guarantee their security within the Chinese system. At the same time they realize that this may just be a romantic hope on their part and hence they must be on their guard even while they long for dependency.

This problem of suspicion and the craving for trust brings up the question of Chinese perceptions of foreign negotiators and the difficulties of accurately communicating with the Chinese. Much of the preliminary phase of hospitality and the exchanging of pleasantries (and the giving of gifts to the Chinese) seems to be calculated to provide the Chinese opportunities to size up the foreign trader so they can determine his reliability as well as his potential negotiating weaknesses. The Chinese are quite aware, however, that people who exude good will in social situations can turn ruthless in business dealings. Hence there is usually a second round of sizing up.

At this stage problems of communication can arise. The early flow of conversation during the initial socialization phase can lead to misjudgments about how well the two parties actually understand each other. Most American businessmen, especially the representatives of large and responsible establishments, are alert to this problem and wisely include their own interpreters in their delegations. The Japanese firms are even more careful, requiring one, and with some firms two, Chinese language specialists to be present in the room whenever serious negotiations are to take place. Chinese foreign language specialists are spread thin, and the Chinese assigned interpreter may have inadequate skills and experience, but the need for one's own interpreter exists even when the Chinese side includes one of their outstanding bilingual translators. The problem is, first, that many nuances may be missed, remarks among the Chinese negotiators will not be taken into account, and clues about Chinese assumptions and misunderstandings will be lost. As Tsuneo Kawasakiya has observed, "The Chinese often express their serious interest with a soft expression."[3]

The presence of Chinese language specialists on a negotiating team opens the possibility for profitable informal exchanges of views outside of the negotiating rooms. It is a standard Chinese practice to seek out such people during breaks in the formal meetings to clarify points, explain what may be on the minds of the Chinese principals, and ask for explanations about the positions of the other side. Frequently, the Chinese hesitate to bring up questions at the formal meetings but are quite prepared, indeed eager, to have informal conferences to work out problems. Above all, the presence of such people facilitates the process of building trust and, by helping to overcome Chinese suspicions, encourages the Chinese response of dependency.

One of the mysteries of official U.S.-China relations is the practice

---

[3]"Organizing for China Trade: The View from Japan," Address to Seminar on Doing Business with the People's Republic of China, Business International Institute/Asia, Hong Kong, April 1979, p. 15.

of American officials of meeting repeatedly with high Chinese officials without the benefit of their own interpreters. Such officials are presumably as anxious to protect the U.S. national interest as, say, Japanese traders are of protecting their firms' interests. They should want to be certain that their own ideas are communicated accurately, that they would be informed about potential misunderstandings, and that they are being told more than what the Chinese interpreters happen to put into English.

The American businessman's high regard for interpreters does not generally include China specialists or students of Chinese culture. Many had been intimidated by such specialists when they were attending workshops on how to do business with the Chinese. Businessmen claim that such specialists give negative or even paralyzing advice, emphasizing things that should not be done or said for fear of offending the Chinese. Many American specialists on Chinese culture are alert only to what might annoy the Chinese and give little thought to ways of getting ahead of them. One businessman described his company's experience in hiring a China specialist:

> His advice was all negative. He never gave us a hint as to how we might have cashed in on the negotiations. Instead he was constantly worried about Chinese feelings and sensitivities. You would have thought from the way he advised us that that bunch of tough Communists who had gone through the Cultural Revolution were a group of delicate, thin-skinned Victorian sewing-circle ladies.

Aside from their own Chinese language employees, the Japanese traders have not sought out academic specialists on Chinese culture, but their reason is the inability of Japanese academics to have any effective relations with either businessmen or bureaucrats.

Most American firms use Overseas Chinese interpreters, mainly from Hong Kong, Singapore, or even originally Taiwan, many of whom worked for American companies before the China opening. Chinese officials tend to look with considerable favor on such Overseas Chinese, believing that they must have feelings of patriotism and are therefore unlikely to cheat the mother country.

This is further confirmation of the hypothesis that Chinese negotiators feel anxious about being cheated and hence will respond readily to whatever offers hope for greater security. The mere presence of ethnic Chinese on a foreign negotiating team leads them to quickly communicate their concerns to such persons. Whether the Chinese perceive the presence of the Overseas Chinese as points for penetration or as signs of friendship, they are welcome for they suggest that negotiating with the particular American team will be less threatening.

Precisely because they see such Overseas Chinese as desirable channels of communication, Chinese cadres often intentionally or unintentionally pressure them in their informal conversations to beg their American employers to accept Chinese positions. The speed with which Chinese try to use such informal channels reflects their cultural presumption that one need not be inhibited in asking favors of even newfound "friends," especially if there is a bond of sentiment in the relationship, such as the bond of a common identity.

American businessmen with Chinese staff members thus find themselves in a peculiar situation. On the one hand they tend to be well received by the Chinese, and they are able to get considerable clarifying information out of them through informal contacts. On the other hand, they find that their interpreters are exposed to considerable pressure as the Chinese make heavy demands of them.

The executive of a substantial American company that has long had a Hong Kong office summed up the advantages and problems in using Hong Kong Chinese as interpreters in these words:

> We were originally a little nervous because both of our key Chinese staff members had fled China to get away from the Communists. To my personal surprise when we went in the first time, we found that the Chinese immediately latched onto them and embraced them in friendship. Consequently, when we started negotiations the Chinese explained all their problems to them and they were able to cue me in on everything. Without them we would have really been in the dark. Soon, however, I realized that the Chinese were putting the screws to them, expecting them to get concessions out of us. I could see that it was a tough situation. We benefited tremendously by their presence, but they were put in a brutal bind. I had to give them strong reassurances that we understood the situation and they should not feel threatened. I knew their loyalties were with us, but they also had their feelings for China.

In spite of their understandable feeling of being more comfortable with someone of their own race, Chinese officials find it hard to believe that Chinese-Americans may in fact be in positions of authority in American firms and actually have command over Caucasian Americans. The notion that a white man's firm should be managed by white people is so strong that Chinese cadres tend to suspect that there is something unnatural about having Chinese-American executives in them.

The Japanese have no such problems because they do not employ Chinese ethnic interpreters. They do report, however, that the Chinese seem to appreciate the presence of people who speak Chinese on the Japanese negotiating teams and that they do seek out these interpreters between sessions to communicate matters they feel constrained not to bring up in the formal sessions.

PROBING FOR AND EXPLOITING THE OTHER'S INTERESTS

Once the negotiating exchange begins the Chinese seem to become surprisingly passive, expecting that the other party will take the initiative in proposing concrete deals. In part this posture may simply reflect Chinese inexperience in international trade, as they allow the other party to be the teacher while they act as students. At the same time, however, the posture seems to be part of a conscious negotiating ploy.

Negotiating sessions thus tend quickly to take the form of the aggressive foreigner trying to arouse the interests of the somewhat withdrawn Chinese. One of the businessmen spoke for the majority when he said,

> In substantive dealings with Chinese it is necessary first to figure out what you have that the Chinese should be interested in; then you have to decide how best to convince the Chinese that it is in their interest to buy, and then you have to just keep selling and selling and selling as hard as you can.

For American companies this usually means that they must somehow convince the Chinese to give priority to the particular things the Americans wish to sell.

The situation for the Japanese is somewhat different in that the large trading companies and the Japanese-China Trade Association representatives are ready to sell and buy simultaneously, and they deal with a far larger range of manufactured items and raw materials. Furthermore, the Japanese companies operate with the backing of substantial Japanese government credits to China. Consequently, the Japanese process of convincing the Chinese that they have things China needs takes place on a broader scale, and the Japanese can more easily adapt their sales to the Chinese basic plans. The Japanese tend to operate more within the context of known Chinese plans, concentrating, for example, on infrastructure developments and total industry planning. They do not have to engage in as vigorous efforts to capture the interests of the Chinese because they begin with Chinese priorities and only then must sell themselves as the appropriate supplier.

The bargaining position from which the Americans start also means that they generally provide more free technological information to the

Chinese than the Japanese do. Proceeding on the assumption that the Chinese cannot modernize until they learn a great deal more about the different fields, American firms are anxious to head the Chinese in the direction of their own unique products. The Japanese, starting with the notion that the Chinese know what they want to buy, only have to convince them that the Japanese are best equipped to satisfy their needs.

In spite of these differences, however, the basic dynamics for both American and Japanese are much the same in that each must take the initiative and try to sustain Chinese interest. Working from their more passive posture, the Chinese have developed a wide array of probing techniques and ploys. The most common is no doubt the classic demand, "You'll have to make a much better offer to get my interest." In Chinese bargaining this ploy usually takes the form of not so subtly hinting that in the future very large contracts may be possible if the other party will begin by giving a good price on a small purchase. Almost to a man, American businessmen engaged in selling to the Chinese reported that at some point the Chinese had asked for such deals, and to a man all insisted that they personally had never signed an explicitly unprofitable contract with the Chinese. (One businessman did say later in the conversation that his company would have to make some big and profitable deals with the Chinese in time because they had already "sunk" several million dollars into "opening the door," suggesting that he in fact had played the Chinese game.)

The Japanese more readily admit that they have made unprofitable agreements with the Chinese, but they insist that they have gotten instant tradeoffs in the form of other and more profitable agreements. Because the large Japanese firms trade in many fields simultaneously, they are, of course, in better positions to balance out their contract negotiations in a shorter time period than American companies with more limited lines to sell.

The great advantage the Chinese have in using this ploy of titillating foreign traders about business possibilities is that traders are excited less by current realities and more by their expectations about future opportunities in China. As long as traders want to be in on China's promising future they will continue to forgo current benefits in hopes of bigger ones later, in spite of all their denials of agreeing to unprofitable short-run deals.

Closely related is another ploy, also much used in China's international relations, of saying "You are a world leader and hence can take all the risks while we at present are still backward." The remark "You are now strong, but in time we too will be great" has the negotiating merit of mixing flattery with apparent candor about one's own abilities. The key to success in this approach is the Chinese insistence that they have the same feelings as the other party but are unable to act because of their stage of development; yet once they overcome their current problems they will proceed along the same lines as they are asking the other party to do now. Several of the American businessmen confessed to being quite taken by the prospect of being in the short run the champions of Chinese development because of the hope that in the long run they would more than pay back the investment.

The success of this ploy seems to lie in a deep-seated Western, and more particularly American, belief that somehow the Chinese deserve a better fate than is now theirs and that in time such a talented, wise, and energetic people will gain their rightful place in the world. Of course, that is not a poor developing country but a highly civilized and clever people.

Not all businessmen accepted the logic of this ploy, and even some of those who did admitted that they were uneasy about China's future. One very thoughtful American confided:

> I have always had this big haunting question in my mind since I came to Hong Kong: Is China any different from India? They both talk great lines; in fact the Chinese now are just like the Indians in harping on their past mistreatments and therefore their future right to greatness. Yet over the years we have poured huge amounts into India and it just fades away, and I wonder if the same is not going to be the case with China. Could it be that one quarter of mankind could suck dry the rest and still wallow in poverty? Or are the Chinese about to prove themselves as a nation to be as intelligent and industrious as the individual Chinese I know? If I only knew the answer to that question I would know better how to negotiate with them.

A closely related Chinese negotiating response to American assertions that the United States has what China needs is their position that "since you are so advanced you must be generous in teaching us." The Chinese are not interested in just buying advanced technology for the sake of increased production because they also see the acquisition of technology as a means for training their own engineers. This goal of learning from those who sell the most advanced technologies has been a constant since the first introduction of the Four Modernizations, but there has been a modification in the Chinese approach. Initially the Chinese were determined to be self-reliant, and they wanted their technicians to figure out the workings of the new technologies with a minimum of explicit instructions. When the British delivered the first Trident aircraft, their engineers were kept in a Beijing hotel room for six months while Chinese aeronautical engineers studied all aspects of the plane and called upon the frustrated Britishers only when they were unable to unravel a problem. The same occurred, but to a less extreme degree, with the Boeing 707s and with the Kellog-Pullman fertilizer plants. Now, however, the Chinese have gone to the other extreme of expecting that any major sale should also include, at no added expense, an extensive training program.

A fourth common approach is the explicit expectation that "If you wish to deal with China you have an obligation to help China in diverse ways." Sometimes this expectation is written into the contract, such as the requirement that the foreign enterprise will insure that China is able to quickly recoup any foreign exchange investment. The expectation, however, usually extends beyond the scope of the contract, as the Chinese seek an all-enveloping, diffuse relationship. Even during the negotiations the Chinese will probe to find out how cooperative the foreign party is likely to be in providing information and guidance. The probe can be either of a very general nature, such as, "In your judgment what is the best way of getting into the European markets," or very specific, such as, "Could you tell us the reputation of such-and-such a foreign firm?" The art of posing such questions can be a test for determining the willingness of the foreign party to be helpful. The process, however, can also be one that opens the door to continuing Chinese demands for help, which can in time become a burden. One American businessman told how he became increasingly entrapped:

> After just about every session I found out that they had raised all kinds of extraneous questions for which I had to telex to New York to get answers. We were becoming an information service for the Chinese, but that seemed to be the price they expected us to pay for their business.

A Japanese trading official, reacting to the same Chinese approach, said, "We are very courteous in answering all of their questions, but we also have to be very careful and only give them the briefest answers possible. The answers have to be accurate or the Chinese will blame you, but they shouldn't be so good that the Chinese will keep bothering you."

The effectiveness of all of these ploys stems from the fact that they all seem to be natural developments in a relationship that brings together the aggressive, self-dramatizing American side and the passive, counteracting Chinese. The analogy of the self-assured male being manipulated by the coy female is illuminating and comes close to the dynamics of the situation. The basic Chinese expectation seems to be that the more aggressive side will sooner or later rise to the bait of committing itself without quids pro quo and after which will come possibilities for further marginal concessions as one shows greater interest in what is being offered.

The Chinese seem to carefully avoid saying anything that might puncture the self-esteem of American negotiators. Indeed, as they egg on the Americans to tell more about what they are capable of doing for China, the Chinese skillfully feed the American assumptions of Chinese backwardness.

OBSTINACY VS. FLEXIBILITY

Most characterizations of Chinese negotiators suggest a strange contradiction: At one moment they are described as being stubborn, firm, and tenacious, willing to wait with Oriental patience for the other side to give in; but they are also said to be realists, ready to adjust quickly to imperatives of human relations, and always anxious to be conciliatory if given a chance. They are thus seen as being both unyielding and highly adaptable, determined to have things their own way, but also considerate of the other side's requirements.

How did the American and Japanese businessmen explain the contradiction? Most agreed that both characterizations were correct, and therefore everything depends upon the circumstances and how the Chinese feel about a particular issue.

The Chinese seem to be obstinate whenever they feel that the "principles" of the relationship are being challenged, their long-range objectives are being compromised, or what is being proposed is not compatible with their current plans. In short, the Chinese posture becomes rigid whenever they feel their own goals are being compromised. This perhaps explains why the picture of the unbending Chinese negotiator appears more often in accounts of Chinese diplomatic behavior than in business negotiations.

The Chinese also quickly adopt a stubborn posture whenever they are confronted with propositions that go beyond the scope of their authority. Usually Chinese negotiators are given little authority and therefore questions must be repeatedly referred back to their superiors. While this is taking place, Chinese negotiators seemingly find it prudent to adopt a negative attitude. At the same time, however, they usually avoid saying anything that might complicate later dealings on the subject. If their superiors authorize them to go ahead they can suddenly become most accommodating. They do not seem to feel any obligation to justify or apologize for their previous stubbornness.

This pattern explains why quite frequently in negotiations Chinese will respond with silence to a proposal and then at a much later date suddenly return to the proposal with considerable interest. Most

American businessmen have assumed that the initial silent treatment meant that their proposal had been killed and that the Chinese were just being courteous by not openly saying so. Those businessmen with more experience have come to expect such reactions, and one even said his whole agenda of proposals was getting the Chinese "silent treatment," but he was optimistic that in time they would respond positively to some items.

The counterpart of this avoidance of the unambiguous "no" is the Chinese practice in diplomatic negotiations of saying that they will "take note of your position" and then suggest that the discussions "go on to another point."[4] Historically Chinese diplomats have preferred to play their cards very close to their chests and suggest inflexibility until the moment of accommodation.

The impression of Chinese flexibility is related to the initial and the terminal phases of the negotiating process. It is thus closely linked to Chinese practices of hospitality at the beginning and to their style in arriving at settlements. At the preliminary stages of trying to reach an agreement on principles, the Chinese act as though "everything will be possible when we get to the concrete arrangements." Also during early social exchanges the Chinese like to convey the impression of being reasonable and accommodating. Once they have reached agreement they convey the impression that success comes about because of Chinese adaptability. Even when their concession is not great they tend to act as though it is. As one businessman reported:

> We had been negotiating off and on for eighteen months and during all of that time it was always we who had to make concessions to keep the Chinese going. But then when we wrapped up the contract in Shanghai, they were all smiles and insisted that they were happy to have made the final necessary concessions to see it all through. They definitely like to make it seem as though it was they who made all the sacrifices.

Chief executive officers are usually involved at the beginning and the final phases of negotiations, and hence it is not surprising that they are most vocal in characterizing the Chinese as pragmatic and reasonable negotiators.

In contrast to this conciliatory posture at the end of negotiations, the Chinese, during the heat of bargaining, seem to view the concept of compromise as tantamount to "selling out." Indeed, the Chinese word for "compromise" has negative overtones in contrast to its positive connotation in English.[5] The Chinese notion is that for any

---

[4]Freeman (1975), p. 11.
[5]Freeman (1975), p. 10.

concession made, one must be gained in return. It was Mao Zedung himself who stressed that in all negotiations the Communists must give "tit-for-tat" in escalating demands or in expecting returns for concessions.

High Chinese officials can more readily make concessions whereas lower officials have to be more careful and hence appear to be stubborn. The higher the official the greater the flexibility. Unfortunately, all too often the high officials are involved only at the initial stage, particularly if the negotiations had been started by chief executive officers, while lower officials are brought in when the hard negotiating begins.

IN HORSE TRADING THERE IS ALWAYS A LOSER

In spite of the somewhat passive posture of the Chinese negotiating teams they do act with alacrity when questions arise about how the benefits of an agreement are likely to be distributed.

Traditional Chinese culture had a well developed appreciation of the value of markets for all involved, and even under Communism the Chinese have demonstrated far greater sensitivity to consumer interests than have the Soviets. Therefore it is somewhat surprising that the businessmen were generally of the opinion that the Chinese believe someone is always a loser in extensive horse trading. Repeatedly they told of their difficulties in convincing the Chinese that the quids and the quos would actually balance out, and that both parties would benefit equally from the agreement. They found the Chinese highly suspicious that they were being outwitted and they seemed comfortable only when their own benefits were manifestly great.

Several of the businessmen attributed this exaggerated sensitivity to the Chinese belief that they were badly cheated by Westerners in the 19th century. To some degree historical memory may play a part, but another powerful factor has to be their more immediate fear of being criticized by their superiors for making a bad deal for China.

In judging whether or not a deal is "bad," the emphasis seems to be not solely on the issue of whether it benefits China, but also on the question of whether the other party's benefits may not be disproportionately larger than China's. In part this attitude may reflect the fact that Chinese negotiators have limited domains of responsibility and are unable to evaluate the relative benefits for China of their particular deal. Their evaluation of tradeoffs has to be concentrated on the question of benefits for the other party. Even if the deal is "good" for China it will be seen as "bad" by the Chinese negotiators if they believe it to be better for the other party. These attitudes appear to stem from more than just bureaucratic anxieties. They reflect deep Chinese rural suspicions of merchants and traders. With the notable exception of some very commercially oriented cadres, usually from Shanghai or Canton, most Chinese officials tend instinctively to believe that everything is a zero-sum game. They are convinced that in any situation there must be a winner and a loser. Even when both are benefiting one will benefit more than the other, hence there is still a loser. The fact that the losing may be a matter of prestige—a problem of "face" and not a substantive loss— does not make it any easier to take.

In responding to this attitude some American businessmen have found it useful to spell out in elaborate detail all the possible benefits for China, to point out the risks, and then to explicitly define what their companies hope to get. The presentation is necessary not so much to convince those in the room but to provide them with the necessary ammunition to protect themselves and to win over their superiors.

EXPLOITING THE FAULTS OF THE OTHER PARTY

As negotiations proceed a standard tactic of the Chinese is to make full use of any liabilities, mistakes, or even misstatements of the other side.[6] Before 1979 if a firm had previous operations in Taiwan, it might expect to be reprimanded for working with the enemy of the Chinese people; since 1979 if the firm ceased its operations in Taiwan, it may be charged with following a "Two China" policy and not recognizing that Taiwan is a province of China. For example, if there is a failure in the negotiations to refer to China as the "People's Republic of China," or if since 1979 *pinying* is not used in romanizing Chinese words, the Chinese are inclined to make an issue, hoping that by putting the Americans on the defensive they will be able to gain some benefits.

Several of the American respondents said that the anxieties the Chinese were able to arouse by such quibbling tactics seemed to be completely out of line with any conceivable objectives. One businessman said,

> When you are in China you are constantly on guard about making any mistakes over which the Chinese might take offense. They are quick to jump on you, correcting what you may have said or done.

[6]Kazuo (1979), p. 533-534.

They seem to feel that it strengthens their hand to do this. But frankly, I don't see what they really expect to gain by making you feel uncomfortable. It can't change the terms of the negotiations. But they sure have to do it. It must make them feel superior.

Several of the American businessmen said that they carefully avoid any discussion of U.S.-China relations in the 1950s and 1960s, but they are aware that the Chinese believe the United States was "wrong" during that whole period. They therefore expect any American to admit to American mistakes if the topic were to be raised. Simply by not talking about U.S. policy the businessmen feel that they are probably suggesting to the Chinese that they tacitly accept their views.

The Japanese report that the Chinese constantly bring up the history of Japan's occupation of China and attempt to embarrass Japanese traders by mentioning past and recent "faults" of the Japanese government. At one time it was necessary for the Japanese to make routine apologies to the Chinese for the past, but since normalization of Japanese-Chinese relations this requirement has mostly disappeared. However, Chinese negotiators still do not hesitate to try to shame Japanese traders with criticism of actions by Japanese political leaders.

No doubt, the Chinese expect that by "shaming" the other party they can cause him to act in a more righteous manner, which to them means a manner more favorable to China, the error-free country deserving of favoritism. Thus the very same psychological sensitivities that make the Chinese such skillful and considerate hosts can be readily brought into play to make the guest feel uneasy.

If a Chinese negotiator feels that he or China has been "mistreated" by someone even remotely connected with the other party he can become extremely aggressive in trying to "shame" that person and extract a "self-criticism" from him.

MAKING UNACCEPTABLE DEMANDS OPENS THE DOOR FOR EXPECTED CONCESSIONS

In the middle of negotiations on details the Chinese seem to have no hesitation in raising what they must understand are unacceptable demands, which, however, they hint can be tabled if only the other side makes some modest concessions. The extremeness of the position is not backed by equally extreme fervor, and once the concession has been extracted the Chinese act as though they had never been unreasonable.

As a part of this ploy the American businessmen are presented with stark demands in the formal sessions but then told informally between sessions, usually through their Overseas Chinese staff member, that there is no need for a confrontation if the Americans would only make a "helpful concession." Clearly the Chinese do not expect their ultimatums to be treated at face value but rather they are trying to say, "Unless you are willing to make a modest change the situation is impossible." They do this by posing the "impossible" and expecting that the "reasonable" will be done. This particular ploy naturally fits the Chinese style of hyperbole. They readily use exaggerated language to describe awful possibilities; yet just a slight change can produce a completely different vocabulary.

CONSTRUCTIVE USE OF TIME

The Chinese practice of stalling and of exploiting the impatience of Americans is well established. They seem impervious to the possibility that time may work against them rather than for them.

There are also other ways in which the Chinese constructively use time for their negotiating advantages. For example, they seem to feel no pressure to respond promptly to the other party's initiatives, but when they make a proposal they expect immediate responses; throughout any period of waiting they constantly complain about American foot-dragging and even suggest that such delays violate the "spirit of the relations."

Here is another example of the Chinese taking as self-evident and legitimate a tilting that blatantly favors them. They expect others to understand that the workings of Chinese authority must be slow, secret, and unpredictable; but they insist that capitalists should be able to make efficient, hence instant, decisions. The explanation again seems to be both institutional and cultural. Once their superiors have given them the go-ahead to make a definite proposal, the negotiating cadres feel under pressure to report the American response promptly. Culturally the Chinese are compulsive in moving toward action once they no longer feel any inhibitions about authority or about threatening others.

Chinese impatience in negotiating is not usually related to the importance of policy priorities but tends more to be associated with an escape from the uncertainties, self-doubts, and anxieties of threatening authority. When high authority indicates the proper course of action, lesser figures need only respond without hesitation; the wish of the master should be the completed act of the servant.

The Chinese are also extremely skilled at pacing negotiations so as to build up pressures on the other side. In the early stages the Chinese can be excruciatingly deliberate, consuming time as though the process could continue indefinitely. As negotiations move toward a climax, they will not only speed up the process but load down the sessions with a heavy burden of items. Suddenly the American teams find that whereas they could not keep the Chinese working beyond five o'clock, the Chinese have raised a host of issues that will keep the Americans busy throughout the night.

Finally, the Chinese know how to use time in the fundamental sense of raising key issues at awkward moments—for example, at late night banquets after the visitors have consumed considerable amounts of *maotai*. Charles Freeman is quite correct in observing that the Chinese are "masters of the creative use of fatigue."[7] Most American businessmen insist that although they welcome the socializing that facilitates the total relationship, they personally never make commitments in such an informal atmosphere or when relaxed with wine. Yet they also confess that they inevitably feel pressured by such tactics and have to respond fairly promptly at the next day's sessions. According to one American businessman,

> The Chinese do not gracefully mix business and pleasure the way Japanese or even Americans do. What they do is to start off pleasure as though there was going to be no business. Then when it is late and you are tired they will suddenly slip in some business and try to to get you to agreeably go along with them. Even when you don't fall for what they are up to, you have to recognize that what they want, they want very badly and they are not likely to drop it.

REPETITION AND GIVING UP WHAT YOU DO NOT HAVE

Those who have negotiated with the Chinese tend to agree that they have great staying powers and almost no capacity for boredom. From Panmunjom through the Warsaw Talks, the Chinese proved that they could endlessly repeat the same arguments without feeling that they might weaken their position by a tedious repetition of the same words. Today in commercial negotiations, although the same spirit of aggression is not behind their stubborn repetition, the approach is not significantly different, and the spirit is more, "If at first you don't succeed, try, try, again."

For current commercial dealings this quality of Chinese negotiating

---

[7]Freeman (1975), p. 21.

most often takes the form of the Chinese refusing to take "no" for an answer. They will repeatedly come back to their original proposals and endlessly ask if the other side cannot reconsider its positions. The fact that progress has occurred since the rejection of the Chinese proposal does not prevent them from unexpectedly raising the issue again.

Whereas the tactic remains the same, in a strange fashion the Chinese habit of dwelling on repetition is not the same today as it was a decade ago. In the past, the fierce determination of the Chinese in stubborn adherence to their positions suggested high dedication and revolutionary fervor. Today the Chinese practice of constantly harping on what they want takes on some of the qualities of begging. Most of the American businessmen who had experienced such Chinese persistence said that after saying "no" once, they found it easier and easier to say it again and again.

In trying to cling to their original position, the Chinese also frequently use the technique of giving up what they in fact do not actually have as an enticement to obtain a concession. In commercial relationships this tactic often takes the form of the Chinese presenting themselves as being magnanimous because they are not, for example, objecting to the firm's practices elsewhere or its decision to make only a modest beginning in its China relationship. The Chinese will then expect a quid pro quo from the firm.

ASYMMETRICAL EMPATHY

Although the Americans are usually the more impatient and aggressive party and the Chinese the more psychologically astute, Americans find it easier to put themselves into the shoes of the Chinese whereas the Chinese seemingly have little concern for the problems of American companies. Both as sellers and as buyers, Americans want to get as complete a picture of China's needs and potentialities as possible. In spite of their extraordinary skill as hosts and their enthusiasm for the theme of friendship, the Chinese seem to have little empathy for the constraints and limitations within which each particular American company must operate.

This lack of empathy creates more than just acts of inconsiderateness; it often works against the interests of the Chinese. Failing to take seriously the problems the American company may have with, say, scheduling production, delivery dates, and the like, the Chinese may insist upon completion dates that can be met only if they paid more for the product than would be necessary if they were more flexible.

In short, when the Chinese push precise demands, they often do so with only their own internal concerns in mind. They expect that the other party should be able to accept the Chinese perception of their priorities. Thus in the formal sessions the Chinese seem to believe that it is entirely proper for them to bring up their problems, if they wish to do so, and they accept as equally normal that the Americans should be attentively solicitous; but they react as though it were a bargaining trick, hence unworthy of serious attention, for the foreigner to try to explain his problems.

The Chinese, however, do not turn an entirely deaf ear to explanations of the problems the foreign party describes, because often in the informal exchanges between sessions and through the mediating role of the Overseas Chinese interpreter they will ask further questions about the difficulties. These inquiries often suggest that the Chinese now have doubts about the foreign firm's capabilities. Maybe the company is not worthy of being a trading partner of China, for the Chinese prefer to deal only with the "best."

This lack of empathy is an irritant for some Americans because it works against one of their basic principles of negotiation. As one executive explained:

> I have always followed the rule of being as open as possible in all negotiations. It is always best when both sides can lay out all their problems on the table and each can understand the concerns of the other. But this is simply not possible with the Chinese. They may encourage you to understand their problems and they welcome your interest as long as they believe you are being constructive. What they simply will not do is to take your problems seriously and act in ways that are helpful to you. If they feel it is at all against their plans they will not adjust anything to meet you half way.

Here again is a pattern in commercial dealings that also arises in diplomatic negotiations: Although it is the Chinese who are most in need of the relationship, it is the Americans who feel the need to walk on eggs so as not to hurt Chinese sensitivities; and, paradoxically, the Chinese are the more insensitive to the other's problems.

MUTUAL INTEREST, NOT COMPROMISE

The dual but contradictory images of the Chinese negotiators as being both inflexible and pragmatic stems in large part from their determined adherence to what they call "principles" and their more adaptable approach to "concrete details." In addition, however, the

Chinese apparently see less inherent merit than Americans do in the concept of compromise, of give and take and of tradeoffs. Instead, the Chinese prefer to hold up for praise ideals of mutual interests, of joint endeavors, and of commonality of purpose.

Although the Chinese understand the need for some degree of give and take and they are skilled at quietly calculating bargaining exchanges, they do not explicitly honor the idea of compromise, an ideal that Americans enthusiastically extol. It is true that the Chinese will continually ask for more than they hope to get, but when they reach the point of settlement they prefer to play down the fact of retreat by both sides and play up the idea that all along both sides have mutual interests that have finally been recognized.

This may seem like an unnecessarily fine shading in meaning, but it is significant in determining proper negotiating tactics in dealing with Chinese negotiators. American businessmen (and probably government officials) generally feel that there is something artificial in professing shared interests, which implies for them a deeper level of commitment. They are more comfortable in saying that they reached a deal through compromises, suggesting a more limited but very concrete coming together that does not prejudge the overall level of mutual interests.

American negotiators tend to play up the record of whatever concessions they have made and demand appropriate quids pro quo for each concession. Starting from a position of enthusiastic over-selling, they find it congenial to pull back to whatever size of deal seems to appeal to the Chinese. The Chinese seem intent on stressing progress in the unveiling of underlying mutual interests. To Americans the acknowledgment by the sides that satisfactory compromises have been made is the last step toward the consummation of negotiations. For the Chinese the acknowledgment that both sides have common interests is only a first step in a continuous process of trying to get the other party to do more for the common interest.

This difference is well illustrated in negotiations about joint ventures, which, in spite of a bad history with the Russians, the Chinese champion in no small part because they formalize the Chinese ideal of first a commitment to mutual interests and then an opportunity for continuous jostling for advantages. American businessmen have been instinctively wary of the very concept of joint ventures, especially when compensatory trade is involved, because they want the compromises spelled out first.

NOTHING IS EVER FINAL

These considerations point to a major difference in Chinese and American negotiating styles: Americans from the outset conceive of the negotiating process as properly leading to consummation when an agreement is reached that will be binding on all parties and provide a given period of fixed and predictable behavior. The Chinese seem to have less feeling for the drama of agreement and little expectation that any formalized contract will end the process of negotiations. Several informants described their surprise that the Chinese brought up proposals for revising what had been agreed upon, right on the heels of signing a contract. Thus although they are reportedly scrupulous in adhering to agreements, they have no inhibitions in proposing changes.

In the same vein Chinese officials do not seem troubled by the thought of suddenly terminating contracts before their completion date if the terms permit it. The cancellation in September 1980 of the agreement to build a $250 million foreign trade center in Beijing after nearly $7 million had been spent is only one dramatic case of such Chinese reversals.[8] Many agreements over the years have come to the same fate, but let it be added that in every case the termination was consistent with the cancellation clauses in the contract.

The Chinese apparently do not believe that even such extreme acts as the cancellation of an agreement should affect relations with the parties involved. In their view, negotiations should proceed while efforts are made to determine anew what are the "mutual interests" of all parties. Although this attitude clearly annoys the Americans affected by it, the lure of the China market almost always brings them back for another try.

Even in the less extreme cases in which there is no termination, Americans seem to experience a mixture of irritation and anxiety over the Chinese refusal to appreciate that closure should have an element of finality about it. The very act of raising new questions after agreement has been achieved introduces uncertainty at precisely the moment when Americans expect bonds of stability. For the Chinese, however, the prospect of continuous bargaining suggests an enduring relationship. For Americans there can be a great deal of give and take before agreement is reached; afterward neither party should lean on the other to seek further advantages. For the Chinese the very achievement of a formalized agreement, like the initial agreement on principles, means that the two parties now understand

---

[8]Fox Butterfield, "New Wariness over China Deals," *New York Times,* October 1, 1980.

each other well enough that each can expect further favors from the other.

For Americans the establishment of a good relationship means that there should no longer be any strains of bargaining when tacit understanding takes over; for the Chinese a good relationship is one in which there is no need for inhibitions in asking for favors, and the other party is not annoyed by limitless demands and requests.

Although the Chinese belief in continuous negotiations is most apparent in post-agreement situations, it also exists in exactly the opposite situations. When Americans have concluded that no agreement is possible because the parties are too far apart, and therefore the end is at hand, they can suddenly be surprised by a Chinese concession that keeps the negotiations going. Just as there is no finality for agreements, so there is no finality for disagreements.

PERSONAL MANNERISMS

Beyond tactics and bargaining methods there are also some noteworthy differences in the personal style of Chinese negotiators compared with the American ideal of proper negotiating manners. There are marked variations among Chinese officials, some of whom conduct themselves in ways that are most winning to Americans and others who can be irritating and even personally hostile. The following characteristics seem to be fairly common.

Above all, the Chinese can be exceedingly polite and dignified. In contrast to the hail-fellow-well-met approach of the upbeat American salesman, the Chinese are instinctively reserved, even as they are touting friendship. Although the Chinese objective may be, indeed usually is, to establish a personal relationship, their approach tends to be far more guarded than that of Americans. At the same time, however, they seem to have longer memories for early casual exchanges and will be quick to suggest at a later date that a relationship had been established in a situation the American may not recollect.

Chinese negotiators do not feel as strong a need as American negotiators do to take command of meetings or try to dominate the discussions. As for the critical question of controlling the agenda, this the Chinese do unilaterally before the actual sessions in which they are prepared to allow the Americans to perform.

The Chinese do attach great importance to accuracy, and hence they will ignore the tone of a meeting and singlemindedly press for clarification, often in a persistent if not rude fashion. When they achieve clarification they usually do not reveal their reactions.

The Chinese will freely ask questions that often go beyond seeking clarification as they try to pick up as much technical or other information as possible. The Japanese have learned that it is best to give simple and direct answers to questions and not try to elaborate on the answers. This is partly because full answers can cause confusion, but also because they sense that the Chinese are frequently looking for free information.

In formal sessions the Chinese tend to be all business. Usually they do not seek to break the tension by small talk. Instead they generally prefer the safety of silence. Several of the American businessmen described situations in which there were periods of prolonged silence as awkward problems surfaced and the Chinese seemed to feel no compelling need to take the verbal initiative. Furthermore, the Chinese seem quite prepared to end a meeting on a negative note, which violates a basic rule of American negotiating practices.

Although the Chinese tend to have large negotiating teams, they are usually very well coordinated, and they do operate as solid units. Americans can often identify different functional responsibilities among the Chinese team members, but none of the respondents said that they had ever had any success in playing off the interests of the different Chinese. Chinese negotiators do not hesitate to stop a session in order to get instructions from their superiors. They are somewhat less inclined to ask for time for caucusing, something American negotiators have no hesitation in doing.

In responding to proposals from the other side, the Chinese frequently appear to be agreeing when they respond by saying that it is "possible." The answer, however, is often an ambiguous way of saying "no."

Finally, possibly the most striking personal characteristic of Chinese negotiators is their ability to separate whatever emotions they may show from the actual progress of the negotiations. Many respondents said that Chinese negotiators never telegraphed their next moves through a show of emotions. The level of friendliness or of impersonality would remain the same whether the negotiations were approaching agreement or failure. Consequently there seems to be a considerable element of surprise in negotiating with the Chinese.

V. THE EMOTIONAL BASIS FOR THE CHINESE NEGOTIATING STYLE

Although much negotiating calls for rational judgments and scheming in the choice of tactics and ploys, the parameters of decisionmaking are strongly cultural. The levels of trust and distrust, of belief in the manipulatability of events, of confidence in considering all contingencies, and the like are all matters that are fundamentally set by the particular culture. The very notion that tacit negotiation is possible in some situations reflects not only a particular cultural predisposition that is inordinately strong among Americans, but it also requires shared cultural orientations to make it work. When the cultural gap between parties is too great, the "logic" of tacit negotiations cannot prevail. Whereas the differences between Americans and Chinese may not always seem so great, in many situations the gap is enough to cause misunderstandings.

Many specific characterizations of Chinese negotiating practices stand in sharp contrast to typical American approaches, such as the Chinese preference for beginning with a generalized understanding in contrast to the American inclination to start with specifics to minimize disagreements. Other themes stem directly from Chinese bureaucratic practices, such as diffusing authority and avoiding responsibility. Yet in almost all cases, what makes Chinese practices distinctive is that they reflect Chinese culture as it has responded to three decades of Communism. This is not the place to try to spell out the configuration of the Chinese political culture now influencing Chinese negotiating styles. However, three major themes do provide the emotional basis for their negotiating style.

THE BLENDING OF XENOPHOBIA AND XENOPHILIA

First, among Chinese, particularly those called upon to negotiate with foreigners, there are widespread and deep feelings of ambivalence about all that is foreign. Pulling in one direction is a mixture of distrust and distaste for the foreign and respect for Chinese traditions and commitment to Chinese nationalism. The combination produces the rarely successfully masked Chinese attitudes of xenophobia.

At the same time, pulling in the other direction, particularly during periods when modernization has been legitimized, is the alluring attraction of the industrialized world, which seems to possess so much that the Chinese desperately want. The haste with which the Chinese have grasped for foreign ways, particularly foreign technologies, and their eagerness, when it is politically safe, to learn about advanced methods are testimony to the surprisingly strong strand of xenophilia in Chinese culture.

The theme of Chinese xenophobia is so well known and the realities of Han chauvinism have been so extensively documented that many people may not be aware of the existence of the counter-theme. Yet Chinese intellectuals have reached for all kinds of foreign ideas, even before the May Fourth Movement, so that the Chinese can also be called xenophiles. There is incontrovertible evidence that Chinese cadres engaged in negotiations have not only tremendous curiosity about foreign ways but voracity for "foreign" things.

Customarily, Chinese seek to resolve their ambivalence over the attraction and repulsion of the foreign by rationalizing that they are only interested to the extent that it may help China to become as rich and powerful as they believe it should rightfully be. Such a formulation, as popular as it has been since the 19th century, is clearly a rationalization. First, there is no practical way of determining what aspects of the advanced industrialized world can be of greatest help for changing China. Like people in all the developing countries, they are confronted with the frustrating fact that no scientific knowledge can tell how societies can be rapidly made into advanced industrial states. If such were so, there would have been many more advanced states a long time ago.

Second, the formulation is a rationalization because people with quite divergent and contradictory interests can use it to justify whatever they personally prefer. Practically every policy advanced in China from the 1898 Reform Movement through the warlord period, the May Fourth Movement, the years of Nationalist rule, even Mao Zedong's "walking on two-legs policy," and now the Four Modernizations have been legitimized by the same argument of using foreign technology to restore and preserve Chinese greatness.

The ambivalence of Chinese negotiators can produce prickly confrontations. At one moment members of a Chinese team can be apparently carried away with enthusiasm for the novelty of foreign products, but suddenly they can turn defensive as they feel the need to assert Chinese superiority. The very process of stimulating excitement about foreign ways can trigger the counter-emotions of Chinese xenophobia. After a Chinese negotiator has lowered his guard and begun to trust the foreign salesman, he may suddenly feel that he has gone too far and that he may be on the verge of becoming a traitor to China's great traditions.

The desire to be seduced by the outside world raises feelings of shame and thereby complicates all the calculations of the negotiations. The tactic of trusting the foreigner gets mixed up with a need for aloofness. The magnet of attraction in things foreign requires a psychological counteraction that becomes, paradoxically, suspicion of foreign motives.

The unconscious awareness that one is both a xenophobe and a xenophile seems to alert Chinese negotiators to the historical propensity of the entire country to vacillate between periods of extreme mass xenophobia and times of relaxation about adopting foreign ways. All cadres are sensitive to the need to protect China's "state secrets" and to be more nationalistic than the next official; yet anyone in a position to be negotiating with a foreign team must have had personal aptitudes that would make him more than normally interested in the outside world, such as an interest in learning a foreign language, developing skills and accumulating knowledge that originated abroad, or just wanting to make China more like foreign societies.

All of this is to say that Chinese negotiators, behind their reserved and poker-faced approaches, are highly susceptible to mercurial sentiments that are easily provoked merely by interactions with foreigners. Many American executives spoke about the sudden changes in the attitudes of those they were trying to do business with, and they universally sought explanations in terms of changes in Chinese policies or reversals commanded from above. Although such may at times have been the reasons for the vacillation in mood, Chinese policies have not been all that erratic. Chinese negotiators were probably often responding to their own internal tensions between liking and disliking the foreigner.

Anyone who negotiates with the Chinese should appreciate the possibility of such a tension. Persistent flattery about China's greatness and its successes will at some point provoke distrust; the opposite approach of dwelling upon all that the outside world has to offer that can help to build China will also provoke distrust. Although the right balance may be extremely hard to achieve, the objective should be a blend that can match the ambivalence of the particular Chinese negotiator. Most likely it will be impossible for foreign negotiators dealing with the Chinese to manage Chinese ambivalences. What can be done is to be sensitive to the problem and not be surprised by changes in attitude and mood.

SCIENCE AND TECHNOLOGY AS RITUAL

Most people called upon to negotiate with the Chinese are aware that their polity has recently gone through a period of great tension between ideology and pragmatism, between "red" and "expert." In rejoicing over the triumph of pragmatism, foreigners may assume that Chinese "pragmatism" means a commonsense, down to earth view of all matters, particularly technological ones. What is often not appreciated is that the Chinese have in the past repeatedly regarded science and technology as potential panaceas for their modernization. Because the Chinese believe that science and technology have almost magical powers, they do not treat these human enterprises as features of ordinary daily endeavors.

In short, there is often a strong element of wishful thinking in the Chinese approach to matters that others see as being merely technical and governed entirely by rational judgments. As a result, the Chinese often expect miracles to come from science and technology. They frequently act as though they believed that by showing proper deference and respectful enthusiasm for advanced technologies they should be rewarded by having their society dramatically changed.

The Chinese desire to have the "best" or the most "advanced" rather than to explore which technologies might be most suitable for their problems directly reflects their view of the symbolic powers of technology. Similarly, they have a propensity to treat technology as though it were self-sustaining, that once a plant has been bought it should be able to perform automatically at its ideal best level, and that little concern need be given to basic maintenance.[1]

Although the Chinese are quite prepared to explore practical considerations in negotiations in great detail, they will with surprising regularity attach inordinate importance to symbolic factors. Those involved in selling technologies to the Chinese report that the standard procedure does not follow the usual Western practice of the buyer explaining what his problems are and asking if the seller has something useful for overcoming the difficulty. Beyond routine statements

---

[1]During 1979-80, various campaigns were carried out against incompetent managers, and frequently they were charged with failure to understand technology; yet often the particular criticisms revealed an equal failure to understand science and technology as social processes. Possibly the most dramatic example was that of the capsized oil rig in Bohai Bay, which resulted in jail sentences for the Director and Deputy Director of the Bureau of Ocean Petroleum Exploration, the dismissal of the Minister of Petroleum Industry, and a "demerit of the first grade" for the Vice Minister. In his letter of "self-criticism" the Minister admitted that he had been "arrogant," "complacent," "impatient," and hence "non-scientific." Other examples abound of the Chinese identifying moral failings as the prime cause of problems in absorbing technology—much as a few years ago they traced failures in revolutionary practices to morality.

about being backward and needing to learn from abroad, Chinese officials rarely describe their practical problems in detail, but rather they focus on what the foreign seller has to offer and how his line compares with that of his competitors. Clearly, those who negotiate purchases feel confident that they can impress their superiors that they have done the right thing if they have favored the "best" over the most practical.

Repeatedly the American businessmen tell of dealings in which the Chinese seemed to be willing to trade utility for symbolic value. A representative of a major American communications systems firm described his experience in these words:

> Our sessions with the Chinese had an extraordinary quality—completely different from anything I had experienced in selling our systems throughout the rest of Asia. At our technical seminars their engineers asked very sophisticated questions and they completely surprised us by how much of the state of the art they knew. Yet it was all very theoretical. They never told us what they really needed or even what their problems were. The bottom line always seemed to be whether we were ready to give them something that was better than anyone else in Asia had. Our engineers had a hard time trying to figure out what they meant by better since they never knew what it was they wanted to accomplish. Elsewhere in Asia they always make us do elaborate studies of what their needs are and how they can best be met. I swear, in Peking they seemed only interested in what would theoretically be the most complex and advanced satellite system available on the market.

Unquestionably, the emphasis upon symbolic values reflects the scarcity of professionally trained negotiating teams and the need to rely heavily upon non-technical bureaucrats. Yet, granted that this is the situation, it is still significant that Chinese officials have this bias toward making technology a highly symbolic matter.

SPINNING A WEB OF DEPENDENCY

It is not an implausible generalization that the most basic emotion Chinese officials bring to the negotiating process is a tension between fear of being severely damaged and a craving for the exhilaration of mastering others. There are repeated examples of how Chinese officials act to protect themselves from the threats of their superiors, and a few of the Chinese delight in tactical maneuvering and the use of ingenious ploys.

Yet at a deeper level, beyond merely manipulating the other party to provide security from criticism and to gain the satisfaction of outwitting others, Chinese officials appear to be working to use the entire process of negotiation to establish some form of emotional bond with the foreign party. It is not just the behavior of the Chinese that suggests this might be the case, there is also the nearly unanimous testimony of the American businessmen interviewed. They felt that during the prolonged negotiations they experienced striking emotions that made them feel peculiarly close to their Chinese negotiating partners. It would be much too superficial to suggest that this might be simply a reaction to Chinese hospitality and courtesy—many Americans found the exaggerated stress on "friendship" a strain, yet at the same time they gradually developed a feeling of bond toward the Chinese. It would be too cynical to say that the Chinese were just manipulating the feelings of the Americans with whom they were dealing for bargaining advantages alone.

It is more likely that the American sentiments were responses to strong Chinese emotions. In their own distinct cultural fashion the Chinese attempt to create emotional ties with their negotiating partners. To some degree they seemed to be asking in a guarded and indirect fashion for help and protection.

Tacitly they had to accept what must have been for them the unpleasant reality that they were compelled to meet the foreigner on grounds where he was unquestionably the superior. The Chinese officials must have, at least unconsciously, treated the foreign negotiating parties in the subtle manner they often use to protect themselves from powerful figures: They would seek security by creating a dependency relationship that would at the same time obligate the powerful to treat them with consideration and not allow them to be hurt. Given their status as Chinese officials they could not openly manifest the explicit modes of deference commonly used in Chinese culture by the weak in their relations with the strong. In particular it would have been inappropriate to use the forms of exaggerated flattery and self-deprecation they customarily use in such relationships. Instead their approach would have to be more subtle, more implicit, and more latent.

Psychologically consistent with what has just been described is the Chinese practice of aggressively denouncing the behavior of another party, accusing it of violating "principles," being "unfriendly," or even being "an enemy of the entire Chinese people," because of things it may be doing with a third party. It is of course partly an exaggeration of the importance of whatever activities they are a part of—a form of Sinocentrism—and relations among all others belong to the periphery of the Chinese world; but the Chinese are also surprisingly insensitive to the dangers of appearing to be impotent, of trying to affect things over which, in the eyes of others, they could have only marginal influence. This behavior reflects a form of dependency, analogous to the way a dependent child expects to get his way by creating an awkward scene. This use of verbal attack, which can be seen as quite insulting, is intended not to break the relationship but oddly to strengthen it. For the Chinese often feel that they can positively influence others by scolding, shaming, and embarrassing them.

The Chinese negotiating style is shaped by the fact that the process involves two levels of negotiations: (1) the manifest level of bargaining about concrete agreements and (2) the latent level at which they are trying to strike "emotional bargains." At the manifest level there are discrete issues calling for agreement or non-agreement; at the latent level there is a continuous flow of emotions as the Chinese seek to build up ever more complex webs of sentiment. The rhythms of the explicit negotiations may have little relationship to the pace at which the personal and human bonds are being nurtured.

Needing to establish a relationship to a tacitly acknowledged "superior" also suggests a heightened awareness of vulnerability. Dependency may provide security, but it can also be risky—hence much tension and suspicion.

Moreover, there is a high potential for resentment, if not bitterness, if the initiative of seeking dependency is not requited by the expected acts of generosity. Again, possibly unconsciously, the official who has assumed the risks of weaving a net of dependency can suddenly become touchy and then hostile if he feels that he is about to be abandoned.

Many of the businessmen reported changes in their relations supporting this line of speculation. A young executive who was selling complex machinery reported:

> I got to know Mr. Wang quite well, and I thought of him as a real friend. He was an older man who had gone through hell during the Cultural Revolution. He didn't want to have any more trouble in life so he was very careful in all the negotiations. He never told me too much about himself or his family, but his way of opening up to me was to ask my advice about more and more things. At first it was just small talk as far as I was concerned; I'd answer his questions off the top of my head; but then I realized it had become very serious. I didn't want to mislead him, but I didn't have the time to do all the research his questions called for. So I tried to break it off a bit, but that didn't work because he quickly got angry. Although he didn't say anything I could tell that he felt I had let him down.

A much older executive with years of working in Japan described his experiences in these words:

> I was used to the Japanese way in which they are very formal and stand-offish at first, but then there comes a moment when they drop

all their guards and just allow their feelings to take over in a sort of drunken fashion. With the Chinese, they also start off in a formal way, but it doesn't last for days because right away they become friendly. But you don't get that complete spirit of open frankness that you do with the Japanese. The Chinese are more like Americans in the sense that they are good at being friendly but it is sort of superficial and you don't really get through to the other fellow. Yet I do think a couple of the fellows I worked with were truly becoming my friends. They began to want to take up all my spare time and they imposed on me in ways the Japanese would never do.

Another older businessman described his relation with Chinese negotiators by saying:

Each time I go back to China it can be embarrassing because someone whom you once negotiated with but have forgotten will greet you as a long lost friend. They'll act as though you had never been away. It is true that during long and hard negotiations you really get to know the other man and you can even begin to like him in more than just an easy-going way. But you know you have to go on to other things and you can't get yourself all tied up with the problems of a particular chap. But that is not the way they are. They expect that when you come back again you will remember everything about them and you'll be ready to become even more friendly. It can get a bit thick, but that is just their way of doing business.

FACE AND GUANXI

The undercurrent pull of dependency among the cadres reinforces two traditional Chinese concepts that present-day Communists would denounce even while manifesting. The first is sensitivity about gaining or losing "face," which focuses on questions of prestige and dignity and reflects surprising vulnerability in self-esteem. Although most cultures recognize that any negotiating process can damage the ego— hence the need for ritualized courtesies—they usually insist that the ideal negotiator be thick-skinned and impervious to personal affronts. In the Chinese culture personal insults and flatteries usually become an integral part of the negotiating process.

Americans can generally understand what might cause Chinese to feel they have lost face. However, it is much harder for Americans to appreciate the Chinese concept of *giving* someone face. It is not that flattery is foreign to American business culture, but rather that Americans rarely see easy compliments in a positive light and feel uncomfortable or even guilty about blatantly building up another's ego.

In Chinese culture the situation is somewhat different. The heavy use of shame as a social control mechanism from the time of early childhood tends to cause feeling of dependency and anxieties about self-esteem, which naturally enough produce self-consciousness about most social relationships. As a result, a great deal can be gained by helping the Chinese to win face and a great deal will be lost by any affront or slight, no matter how unintended. It is well to remember that the Chinese concept of sincerity is the stark opposite of the American concept, in that the Chinese believe that they can manifest sincerity only by adhering carefully to prescribed etiquette. In a sense they are saying, "I will show my sincerity in my relations with you by going to the trouble of being absolutely correct toward you so that you will be happily untroubled about any matters of face."

Coupled with the Chinese concern about face is their concept of *guanxi*—a word for which there is no English equivalent. It can be described as a special relationship individuals have with each other in which each can make unlimited demands on the other. *Guanxi*, which is closely linked psychologically to the Chinese sense of dependency and of face, rules that if there is some kind of a bond between two people—whether as close as blood relation or as distant as being classmates or coprovincials, or even having grandparents who were friends—then each can tax the other and expect automatic special consideration.

The extraordinary emphasis Chinese negotiators place on friendship can be understood only in the context of *guanxi*. Friendship in Chinese culture is not just a positive sentiment, it means sharing *guanxi*; and therefore it implies the certainty of getting a positive response to requests for any special favors that may lie in the province of another to grant. Although Chinese culture is second to none in recognizing the importance of hierarchy in social relations, the concept of *guanxi* is not exactly the same as the patron-client relationship in other cultures because the positive feelings for dependency are so strong in Chinese culture that the subordinate in fact has nearly unlimited rights over the superior. Indeed, the the tilt of advantage often goes to the weaker or poorer partner in a *guanxi* relationship. Chinese exchanges about being more humble and inadequate are not meaningless rituals of false modesty because the person cast as the superior can become deeply obligated. Even more critical, the partner who intimates that he will try to be helpful has, in Chinese eyes, taken on a commitment of *guanxi*.

Consequently, the driving purpose behind much of Chinese negotiating tactics is the goal of creating a relationship, characterized as friendship, in which the American partner will feel strong and not precisely limited bonds of obligation toward the Chinese. Furthermore, once the American negotiators fall into the patterns of *guanxi,* then the Chinese feel completely justified in complaining if the Americans do not deliver the expected benefits appropriate in such a relationship. The Chinese instinct is to press for the full commitment implicit in *guanxi.* Within the American concept of friendship an inability to be helpful in one way can be compensated for by thoughtfulness in another; but in the context of Chinese *guanxi* such tradeoffs are inappropriate and, indeed, are of questionable morality. Hence, it is quite natural for Americans to believe that the Chinese authorities might be, or even should be, placated about arms sales to Taiwan if the action is coupled with expanded offers of sales to Beijing; but according to the Chinese concept of *guanxi* the Chinese will expect that with every sign of improved relations between the United States and China, there would have to be an equal decline in U.S.-Taiwan relations.

All of this is to say that from the beginning of negotiations the Chinese emphasis on friendship, on seeking out the best, and on asking for help while being easily offended are not trivial matters of conviviality and camaraderie or of unfortunate misunderstandings, which Americans often assume them to be. On the contrary, the Chinese are usually singlemindedly trying to build up a relationship in which they will seek to obligate and to shame the Americans into providing special, indeed exceptional, considerations for the Chinese.

The Japanese informants were willing to be very explicit in identifying the importance of *guanxi* as being helpful in establishing a negotiating relationship. As one of the representatives of a major trading company explained: "The Chinese are still Chinese, and of course they want to build up special personal relationships. They still know what *guanxi* is." Yet, strangely, the Japanese response seems to be one of pulling back and resisting any overtures for the ties of *guanxi* by seeking to be more businesslike and impersonal than most American negotiators.

This Japanese behavior is paradoxical because traditional Japanese culture abounds with sentiments comparable to the Chinese feelings of *guanxi*—indeed this was why they could speak with more insight about *guanxi* than the Americans who were generally unacquainted with the concept. Possibly the explanation for the Japanese claims of resisting establishing *guanxi* relations with the Chinese was precisely that they recognized such sentiments and identified them with old-fashioned, traditional ways of behaving, which they now scorn. The Japanese may have felt compelled to prove themselves, in both their own eyes and in those of the Chinese, to have outgrown such "backward" ways and become truly modern men, which the Chinese should also try to become. Their cultural closeness may have made the Japanese try to prove that they were no longer troubled by such feelings.

It is also possible that the Japanese, being more knowledgeable about *guanxi,* which is close to their feelings of *on* and *giri,* have instinctively sought to avoid entrapment because they can foresee the burdens of future obligations or the risks of future disappointments to the Chinese. *On* and *giri* imply a more explicit sense of indebtedness and obligation than the diffusely binding Chinese concept of *guanxi,* which may have made the Japanese wary of getting too close to the Chinese.

Speculation aside, the facts are that American negotiators allow themselves to respond to the Chinese search for so-called *guanxi* relations, while the Japanese are much more sensitive to the potential dangers of backlash by a people whose wishes for dependency cannot be gratified.

VI. SOME NEGOTIATING PRINCIPLES

The purpose of this study is not to produce a strategy plan for negotiating with the PRC. The goal throughout has been to examine the experiences of private sector negotiators as a way of identifying Chinese practices that may help avoid misunderstandings and be useful for governmental negotiations. The act of negotiation precludes any fixed strategies, because each effort at negotiation is influenced by such variables as the specific issues involved, the nature of the initial problem, and the general political context within which the exchanges are to take place.

Yet it is appropriate to single out a few points as general guidelines, particularly those related to the emotional approach the Chinese bring to negotiations.

The Rule of Patience. As noted several times, informants repeatedly counseled the need for patience. Usually, their explanation for this requirement was based on straightforward assumptions:

1. The Chinese must have time to get and to digest all the information they need.
2. The Chinese bureaucracy is sluggish, and decisions are slow in coming.
3. Chinese officials doing the negotiating don't like to strain themselves and won't work overtime.

Other explanations for the need for patience come from cultural considerations (and particularly pertain to the Japanese):

1. The Chinese have a long-range view of things and therefore are in less of a hurry.
2. The Chinese want to be exactly sure of everything and avoid all possible mistakes.
3. The Chinese distrust fast talkers who want to make quick deals.

No doubt these and other similar explanations are valid for justifying the importance of this rule of patience. However, the need for patience is linked at the most fundamental level to the Chinese need for time to weave the distinctive relationship they seek in the negotiation process. It takes time for them to convince themselves that any particular relationship is going to flower in the manner they wish it to. They can decide quickly that some people are not worthy of knowing better, but the decision to "invest" in a relationship cannot be hurried.

On this score Americans, particularly career civil servants, are prone to believe that negotiations between institutional interests can be quickly and impersonally carried out. Officials of various parts of the U.S. government believe they ought to be able to negotiate directly with their counterparts in the Chinese government with few preliminaries and no assistance from mediators in the American mission who have built up personal reputations with the Chinese. Such an approach does not take into account the Chinese need to construct a firm relationship.

The Principle of Restrained Steadfastness. In using time to develop personal relations it is imperative to avoid any inclinations toward escalating personal involvement. Americans generally believe that human relations cannot stand still; if they are not being reinforced and progressing toward greater intimacy, they will stagnate and wither. The Chinese accept that relations can remain on the same level for indefinite periods of time. What they want is a sense of reliability, not just greater warmth.

Above all, the Chinese seem to want the negotiation process to produce a relationship with the aura of permanence. In Chinese culture, as in many others, permanence is not associated with effusiveness, a quality Americans often feel is important in signaling the desire for better relations. It is easy to document that the most successful negotiators with the Chinese have been men who take an optimistic but reserved approach in their personal interactions with the Chinese and who provide ample evidence that they will be around for the indefinite future. Their commitment to trying to learn the Chinese language, to living in Asia, to taking up residence in China, all suggest to the Chinese that they are likely to be steadfast and reliable. U.S. government negotiating teams should always have some such individuals on them. Although the Chinese may be quick to say that someone is an "old friend," and although Americans enjoy calling Chinese "old friends," the Chinese notion of true old friends is one based on a blend of dignity and pleasure.

The Trap of Indebtedness. Closely related is the rule of being cautious about the Chinese propensity to induce a sense of indebtedness to them as a way of achieving what they consider to be secure agreements. Sometimes the emphasis will be at the personal level as they seek to use the obligations of friendship and hospitality. At other times the ploy will be at a more general and historical level, as when they suggest that others "owe" Chinese special considerations because of Chinese interpretations of the past.

Negotiators need to be conscious of whatever obligations they may be accepting from the Chinese, and they need to avoid adding to the

Chinese perception of their readiness to admit indebtedness by effusion of friendship and national self-criticism. There is great danger in misunderstanding the degree of mutual dependency that Americans and Chinese assume exists in any relationship.

Preventing Exaggerated Expectations. Possibly the most difficult guideline for Americans to follow is that of avoiding any encouragement to the Chinese to have exaggerated expectations of what the American side can ultimately supply to China. The American style of exuberant salesmanship, which Americans assume to be no more than harmless friendliness, the Chinese can read to mean that the American is prepared to do more than he intends. The result will be Chinese disappointment and then bitterness.

Although it is no doubt a good general principle not to create unrealistic expectations in others, this is an especially critical problem with respect to the Chinese, who expect high rewards for their own acts of dependency. Once they assume that a relationship has been established they genuinely count on various degrees of generosity, especially if they perceive that the rich and the strong can help them with their difficulties. If they sense that they are not getting all that they feel is their right, then they are likely to become suspicious of the motives and the morality of the other party.

An act of generosity that the Chinese may refuse to accept when it is offered creates the expectation in the Chinese mind that at some subsequent time they have a legitimate right to ask for assistance. The Chinese calculus of "face saving" makes them feel it appropriate to turn down initial offers, but that same calculus says that there is no loss of face to ask for help later. This view is quite different from the American approach in which it is easier to respond positively to another's initiative of generosity than later to ask independently for support. The American calculations of appropriate quids pro quo also tend to use a shorter time frame than the Chinese.

Resist Efforts at Shaming. Whenever the Chinese are disappointed in the follow-up of negotiation, their reactions tend not to be a search for appropriate substantive counter-moves, but rather to attempt to shame the other party by moralistic appeals and denunciations. A case in point is their tactic of first gaining an agreement on general principles and then suggesting that the other party is violating such principles if the negotiations on concrete details do not adhere to the Chinese interpretation of those principles. This approach permeates Chinese relations with others and reflects their traditional belief that others can be controlled by shaming them. The Chinese seem willing to exaggerate the threat to the relationships established by negotiations because they genuinely believe that if the other party can be shamed into doing the "right" thing they will be grateful and not resentful. It does not, therefore, usually occur to the Chinese that criticisms of the other party, even to the point of questioning their integrity, might completely undermine the relationship or leave deep feelings of resentment, even if the Chinese get their way on the matter at issue.

When the Chinese do turn to the tactic of shaming they can be surprisingly easily satisfied by symbolic responses that do not affect the substance of what has been done. An admission that what was done may not have been proper can by itself satisfy the Chinese without the need to retract the action, which the Chinese can now recognize as belonging to the past. They can now go back to the goal of spinning the web of dependency. It is true that in their politics the Chinese have long memories for revenge, so that when someone is under attack incidents of years before quickly surface in emotional outbursts; but in practical terms what is more significant is that the parties had apparently enjoyed harmonious relations during all the intervening years. If the basic relationship is broken then the other party can expect to be viciously denounced for all manner of things he assumed had been patched up. (Some of the Japanese trading companies apparently make a routine practice of being apologetic and making amends for wrongs they have not committed, thus building even stronger relations with the Chinese.)

Take General Principles Seriously. The Chinese usually prefer to begin with agreements about general principles before moving to concrete items, and Americans like to begin with specific matters and avoid generalities. If the objective is to have a successful, continuing relationship with the Chinese, it is usually necessary to follow their route. But in doing so it is imperative to decide ahead of time the precise general principles one is prepared to accept.

It should be possible to preserve the degree of flexibility that Americans are most comfortable with by including in the general agreement contingency considerations as to stages in the advancement of the relationship. That is, the principle can describe a dynamic relationship and not a static pattern. At the same time, however, it is essential to avoid any formulation of general terms one is likely to want to change subsequently. Knowing that the Chinese are likely to use one's commitment to the general principles as a form of pressure at later points in the relationship, one must be comfortable with the general agreement.

Master the Record. Even though the Chinese will change the personnel on their negotiating teams, it is certain that the Chinese negotiator at any moment will be completely knowledgeable about all that went before; and insofar as it is to their advantage to do so they will test the other side's memory. At times they have been known to distort what was previously discussed in order to take advantage of new negotiators. One should therefore keep an exact record of all discussions and not accept the Chinese record as accurate. The Chinese will not feel embarrassed for having their statement of record corrected. They engage in such testing partly because they believe foreigners are by nature careless and deserve to be penalized for their slipshod ways. Thus, instead of feeling guilty for being caught at distorting the record, the Chinese will admire someone whose mind is concentrated on all the details.

Damage Limitation Measures. Inevitably it will at times be necessary to adopt positions that the Chinese find offensive and that violate their beliefs about how people with mutual interests should behave. When this happens the rule is to concentrate on limiting the damage and above all not to engage in mutual recriminations. Those will only convince the Chinese that Americans are indeed insincere. For reasons basic to their culture the Chinese have a stronger need than most people to publicize what they perceive as mistreatment. Although they often hesitate to denounce the source of their consternation outright, they will let the word get around that they are unhappy, and why. When such a situation develops, the rule should be to avoid an aggressive defense at all cost. It would be better to pass the matter off as an unavoidable misunderstanding about which the Chinese have a right to be upset. Even when it is possible to show that the Chinese are in the wrong, it may be counterproductive to point this out, especially when the Chinese are savoring the emotions of perceived mistreatment. Often nothing is called for—for the Chinese, of all people, know the meaning of impassivity.

A review of both the Sino-Soviet and the Sino-Vietnamese splits shows that both the Soviets and the Vietnamese made the mistake of aggressively countering Chinese complaints and thus escalating the tensions between themselves and the Chinese. Rather than seeking to limit the damage of misunderstandings they sought self-vindication. The test for Americans will be whether we can avoid such temptations when the Chinese, as they inevitably will, seek to claim that we have mistreated them.

Know Chinese Cultural Differences But Be Yourself. A final basic principle, which applies to negotiating in all foreign cultures, is almost a truism, but deserves mention: Know the other culture, be sensitive to its distinctive characteristics so as not to unintentionally offend, but also be true to your own cultural standards. Effective negotiating requires a constant alertness to the distinctive qualities of the Chinese to appreciate the meaning behind their actions, so as not to be misled or to mislead them. Yet, at the same time, one can only act superficially in accordance with the rules of Chinese culture. It is impossible to out-Chinese the Chinese. It is also foolish to try to, for the Chinese have had long experience in dealing with foreigners, and Chinese negotiators fully understand that foreigners are culturally different.

Relevance to Governmental Negotiations. Although these summary generalizations about how to negotiate with the Chinese derive from commercial practices, they do have direct relevance for government-to-government negotiations. Indeed, in some respects the above advice is even more relevant for government-to-government negotiations. For example, the rule of patience is probably more applicable in that there are usually few costs associated with the loss of time in governmental negotiations, and the Chinese will be alert to exploit any natural American inclination to impatience.

Cultural proclivities have greater room for play in governmental negotiations, because they lack the unambiguous market imperatives of price, costs, supply, and demand that preside over commercial negotiations. Furthermore, governmental negotiations usually contain a symbolic dimension that can be far more significant than the substance of the finally negotiated agreement. More significance will be attached to how agreements are perceived and interpreted by others than in commercial transactions. Questions will be raised as to whether general principles of reciprocity were respected. Did one party obviously benefit more than the other? Who was the bold party and who the timid? What does any new agreement represent in light of the previous negotiations? In short, the context for governmental negotiations is always highly political, and the results will be the subject of speculation not only in the two countries but in other countries throughout the world.

Chinese political and diplomatic negotiators have consistently displayed the same astuteness that Chinese commercial negotiators have in using their interpretation of the spirit of agreed general principles to influence negotiations on substantive details. Chinese negotiators will not hesitate to question the basic motives of the American side to press their current objectives. The psychology of dependency will lead them to make heavy demands and to feel that they have been mistreated, and even abandoned, if they fail to get their desired responses. Yet they also are capable of understanding that their every wish cannot be fulfilled.

Thus it is appropriate to be firm but understanding, to appreciate Chinese wishes but to adhere to American national interests. In recent years a great deal of the frequent frustration of American negotiators has come from resentment about the way Chinese concentrate almost entirely on their own objectives while discounting all American problems. A healthier relationship requires both sides to take the problems of the other more seriously. Even while resisting Chinese bargaining ploys Americans must recognize the danger that the Chinese will push for what they see as their rights up to the point of being self-damaging. In Chinese culture it is understood that a person may commit suicide to shame someone.

The Chinese tend to adopt a broad definition of self-interest, and of the scope of mutual interests, which means that there is a large zone of issues that may turn out to be quite negotiable. However, some will unaccountably become a trigger for masochism. It is usually quite impossible to judge ahead of time which issues the Chinese will blow up in an apparently irrational, self-destructive manner. The source of the trouble may be an inner bureaucratic matter, perhaps no more than the pride of an official.

Because the Chinese can cause so much trouble for themselves, as well as for others, over what may seem to be only symbolic matters, it is imperative to use extraordinary care in designing appropriate strategies in negotiations with Chinese officials. It cannot be assumed that good will and a sense of shared material interests will be enough to prevent what can become unmanageable problems, particularly because the Chinese have such an instinct for shaming others into believing that they must be the cause of all difficulties.

INDEX

ABOUT THE AUTHOR

Lucian W. Pye, one of the nation's leading authorities on the politics of Asian countries, is Ford Professor of Political Science at the Massachusetts Institute of Technology and a consultant to the Rand Corporation. He has been an advisor on foreign affairs to the Department of State and the National Security Council, a member of the Board of Directors of the Council on Foreign Relations and of many organizations concerned with U.S.-Asian relations. For a decade he was chairman of the influential Committee on Comparative Politics of the Social Science Research Council.

Professor Pye is a political psychologist whose analyses illuminate the fundamental impulses of Asian cultures and their reflection in contemporary Asian political ideology, political values, and political behavior. A major theme in his researches has been the impact of modernization on traditional Asian societies. With intellectual roots in anthropology, psychology, and psychoanalysis, as well as political science, Professor Pye has compared the political behavior and political cultures of Asian nations, including both China and South and Southeast Asian countries, in numerous published works.

Lucian W. Pye is the author of:

> *The Dynamics of Chinese Politics*
> *Mao Tse-Tung: The Man in the Leader*
> *China: An Introduction*
> *Aspects of Political Development*
> *The Spirit of Chinese Politics*
> *Politics, Personality, and Nation Building*
> *Warlord Politics*
> *Guerrilla Communism in Malaysia*
> *Southeast Asian Political Systems*

and the editor of:

> *Communications and Political Development*
> *Political Culture and Political Development* (with Sidney Verba)
> *Political Science and Area Studies*
> *Political Power and Communications in Indonesia*
>   (with Karl D. Jackson)
> *The Citizen and Politics* (with Sidney Verba)

SELECTED LIST OF RAND BOOKS

Liu, Ta-Chung, and Kung-Chia Yeh. *The Economy of the Chinese Main-
land: National Income and Development, 1933-1959.* Princeton, N.J.:
Princeton University Press, 1965.

Moorsteen, Richard, and Morton Abramowitz. *Remaking China Policy:
U.S.-China Relations and Governmental Decision-Making.* Cambridge, Mass.: Harvard University Press, 1971.

Pye, Lucian W. *The Dynamics of Chinese Politics.* Cambridge, Mass.:
Oelgeschlager, Gunn & Hain, Publishers, Inc., 1981.

Quade, Edward. *Analysis for Public Decisions,* 2nd ed. New York: North
Holland, 1982.

Robinson, Thomas W. (ed.). *The Cultural Revolution in China.* Berkeley
and Los Angeles: University of California Press, 1971.

Solomon, Richard H. (ed.). *Asian Security in the 1980s: Problems and
Policies for a Time of Transition.* Cambridge, Mass.: Oelgeschlager,
Gunn & Hain, Publishers, Inc., 1980.

Williams, J. D. *The Compleat Strategyst: Being a Primer on the Theory
of Games of Strategy,* rev. ed. New York: McGraw-Hill Book Company, Inc., 1966.